WEST HEAVENS

从西天到中土

印度新思潮读本

Readers of Current Indian Thought

迪佩什·查卡拉巴提读本 Dipesh Chakrabarty Reader

南方日报出版社
NANFANG DAILY PRESS

《从西天到中土：印度新思潮读本》系列

1《萨拉 · 马哈拉吉读本》

2《帕沙 · 查特吉读本》

3《杜赞奇读本》

4《阿希斯 · 南迪读本》

5《特贾斯维莉 · 尼南贾纳读本》

6《迪佩什 · 查卡拉巴提读本》

7《霍米 · 巴巴读本》

8《吉塔 · 卡普尔读本》

《印度新思潮读本》系列是“从西天到中土”学术项目出版计划的第一组丛书，是专为以下系列论坛编辑的参考读本：

从西天到中土：印中社会思想对话

项目总监：张颂仁

学术主持：陈光兴 高士明

主　　办：第八届上海双年展 中国美术学院展示文化研究中心

承　　办：汉雅轩 梦周文教基金会

支　　持：民生现代美术馆 民生当代艺术研究中心 印度驻上海总领事馆 南方日报出版社 翠菊基金会 邓永锵

特别媒体支持：《南方周末》

West Heavens: Readers of Current Indian Thought

1. Sarat Maharaj Reader
2. Partha Chatterjee Reader
3. Prasenjit Duara Reader
4. Ashis Nandy Reader
5. Tejaswini Niranjana Reader
6. Dipesh Chakrabarty Reader
7. Homi Bhabha Reader
8. Geeta Kapur Reader

Readers of Current Indian Thought is the first series of publication of the West Heavens Project, which coincides with the following academic forums:

West Heavens: India-China Summit on Social Thought

Commissioner: Chang Tsong-Zung

Lecture Curators: Kuan-Hsing Chen, Gao Shiming

Presented by: The 8th Shanghai Biennale, Institute of Visual Culture (China Academy of Art)

Co-presented by: Hanart TZ Gallery, Moonchu Foundation

Supported by: Minsheng Art Museum, The Institute, Consulate General of India in Shanghai, Nanfang Daily Press, Verdant Foundation, David Tang

Media Partner: *Southern Weekly*

缘起

《从西天到中土》是一个综合的文化交流方案，由中国美术学院展示文化研究中心和香港汉雅轩发起，梦周文教基金会资助研究，从学术思想和当代艺术两个角度去亲近印度，进行视觉文化和亚洲现代性的文化比较。读本中的学者于2010年秋的上海双年展期间陆续来华演讲；为了让听众进一步了解他们的思想，每位学者为我们精挑了这个选集，以中英双语出版。

当今的印度离我们既近且远，除了被西方传媒渲染的新兴经济的龙象之争和模糊偏见之外，印度不在一般国人的视野之内。印度咸称古国，但作为当代文明，一个甚至在现代西方思潮中举足轻重的印度学界，并不在普遍意识之中。作为人口的大国和现代国家，印度的经济、文化、科技皆有不可估量的前景；作为中国近邻与久远的故交，印度早就应该被中国关注。但与印度交流的当务之急不在于此；中国须要深切思考印度、亲近印度是为了自明。

中国走上现代化的道路已逾一世纪，从革命到冷战到自由资本全球化，我们的道路一直摆脱不了欧美的世界想象，话语也固定在“东西”和“中西”之说法。无怪中国百年来的各种自强运动的结果，都脱不离西方制度的模式。作为典范的欧美，中国钦羡为“先进文化”，于今天的国情已不适宜无条件借鉴。但面对中国的历史资源时，我们又往往囿于欧美范式而无法善用。如何在冷战的两种西方历史计划以外找到中国的位置，如何发掘被欧美视野冷落的历史资源，就必须放眼其他的发展经验。在亚洲现代化道路上与中国采取截然另途，但依我们的“富强”尺度又是成就可观的例案，无法不审视印度。

中国引以自豪的现代之路是民族革命，彻底推翻过去，重新再造大一统，但结果我们离自己的历史文化越来越远。印度的道路则是摆脱殖民帝国，但在民族独立后依然承继了殖民时代机制。然而，当中国的“后革命”经验与印度的“后殖民”相遇时，我们又不能不讶于左翼革命在印度至今不衰的事实。目前各种倾向的共产党在印度尚有四十多个组织，革命经验不可说不丰富；可是印度又是世上最大的民主国家。这让我们无法不想：中国的革命是否潜伏了殖民基因；而印度的“后殖民”是否革命的另一种方式。印度现代化的历程之多样与丰富，中国无法相比；同时，在日常生活的层面，新旧文化传统并行不悖。雅利安文明的婆罗门学者和各式传统修行人似乎与工业文明不相涉地穿插在都市节奏之中。现代中国与印度相遇，感观上最受刺激的疑惑是：现代与历史（而且是多层面的历史）到底如何并存?

印度与中国的现代都因承欧美的帝国主义和资本逻辑而致，所以中印的相遇是设在欧美的大平台上，绕开欧美无法谈亚洲的现代，也无法深切交流双方的经验。但要脱略于欧美的历史经验来重新自明，不能够自闭地缅怀过去；要打开未来，我们更必须能把中国经验提升为足以让欧美也能借鉴的新知识。这可能是印度当代学术最值得国人参考的一面。这系列读本的作者大多为西方学界熟悉，而且，印度学者擅长的“后殖民”理论和城市研究至今尚是西方新思潮的显学；比方在当代艺术的领域，就直接影响了近二十年的国际趋向。

《从西天到中土》的计划源于展示文化研究中心历年的一系列工作计划。2003 年许江院长倡议以“亚洲”作为中国美术学院建校七十五周年纪念的议题，嘱高士明、吴美纯两教授主持，邀我并预其事。“亚洲的双重时间”从亚洲各国的民间历与耶稣历的并行现象着墨，作为《地之缘：亚洲当代艺术的迁徙与地缘政治》越域考察和展览的基础。2008年广州三年展由高士明，萨拉·马哈拉吉和我策划的《与后殖民说再见》再次启动了对“东西”二元框架的反思。《从西天到中土》企图推进前此的探索，在亚洲内部作近距离和实质的交往。陈光兴教授在这领域已投入多年的气力，承不弃，介入高士明和我的行列，策动了他在学术圈的老关系，论坛才得以顺利成事。此中的心意非言谢可以相报，亦惟有以谢忱言表。为组织和翻译这系列读本投入了大量热情工作的陈韵、彭嫣菡是此项计划的枢纽；并感谢陈恒、孙田审慎的审译，杜可柯、卢隽婷、叶富华、王立秋、张博、戴维佳、林盼盼、钟添雅、夏河、冯盈、曹艺馨和彭嫣菡等的译文，苍穹文化及唐锁的版面设计，南方日报出版社何灿先生和阮清钰编辑的支持，以及民生现代美术馆和民生当代艺术研究中心对出版的赞助，在此谨致谢意。

印度和中国在现代境遇中相遇，不独是现代西化大潮的因缘。远在西风东渐之前，中土唯一一次文化大变革来自汉唐的佛教东渡。佛学来华虽然远远未有近百年西洋革命的残酷惨烈，但其影响之深远，也要历数百年的反刍，直到宋代才被彻底消化。在百年西化的意识形态革命之后，再访天竺可以提醒中国自我改造的历史记忆，并提醒我们在想象世界版图的“西方”时，尚有一个离感官更远而脚程更近的“西天”。

张颂仁记于二〇一〇年八月

Passage to West Heavens / Chang Tsong-Zung

WEST HEAVENS is an initiative for cultural exchange developed jointly by the Institute of Visual Culture of China Academy of Art, and Hanart TZ Gallery, and supported by the Moonchu Foundation. The aim is to foster closer understanding of India through contemporary art and scholarship, and develop cross-cultural dialogue based on visual culture and notions of Asian modernity. Scholars represented in this series of Readers have been invited to lecture at the 2010 8th Shanghai Biennale, and they have specially selected this anthology of representative writings to introduce their thinking to the Chinese public.

Modern India is both near China and far away. Apart from vague generalizations, and supposedly Indian-Chinese economic rivalry enthusiastically promoted by Western media, most Chinese people are unaware of India. Of course we are aware of India's rich history, but we are less familiar with its modern culture, in particular the significant role that played by Indian thinkers in international academia. As China's neighbor and traditional ally, India has long been deserving of China's attention. As a large modern nation, India also has tremendous economical, cultural, and technological potentials. But the most important reason for China to connect with India is to enlighten ourselves.

China has been possessed by the demon of modernization for over a century. From revolution to Cold War, and now capitalist globalism, China has been unable to shake off paradigms set by the West. Even Chinese discourse about modernity has so far been trapped by dichotomies of "East/West" and "China/West". No wonder that efforts at developmental self-reliance have only led to increasingly westernised economic and political institutions and lifestyles. Today the West that China emulates as the model of "advanced civilization" is no longer suitable for guidance. And yet access to China's own historical resource has been blocked by the framework of these models. To establish a position for itself outside the two Western Cold War ideological paradigms, to develop historical resources beyond Western ideals, China must make connections elsewhere. Among Asian countries that have struck off on different paths but still successful by the parochial standards of prosperity, India has much to offer its neighbors.

China's path to modernity has been moulded by a series of revolutions, having overthrown shackles of the past to create new social forms. The damage of revolution is to become increasingly removed from our historical roots. India has adopted radically alternative ways. India overthrew colonial domination, but characteristically preserved colonial institutions after liberation. And yet, when China compares its post-revolutionary record with the post-colonial experience of India, we can't help but be amazed at the prevalence of left wing politics in India. There are currently over forty major parties of Communism in India, engaged in varying forms of revolutionary tactic. At the same time India is also impressively the world's biggest democracy. China's encounter with India inadvertently raises the suspicion: whether if China's revolution harbors a latent colonial gene? Conversely, whether the Indian version of post-colonialism is in fact another form of revolution? China's singularity of state purpose has completed the most daunting social engineering in history; but in terms of diversity and richness of historical culture it is no match for the treasure trove of India, where old and new traditions co-exist on the level of daily life. Brahmins and Sadhyus of ancient descent have integrated into the fabric of industrial urban life. In the modern encounter of two ancient civilizations, an urgent issue is being raised for China: How do modernity and history, history with multi-layered complexity, coexist?

Both the modernity of India and China have been shaped by Western imperialism and capitalist logic, so the modern meeting of India and China cannot but be under the auspices of the West. Asian modernity cannot be understood, no profound inter-Asian exchange is possible outside of this context. And yet, to go beyond the experience of the modern West, to return to our own histories, a myopic obsession with the past is unrealistic. To truly open up the future, local history and reality must be shown to have global significance. For China this is perhaps the most valuable lesson of our Indian colleagues. The authors collected here are not only well versed in Western academic discourse, their own work have made major contributions worldwide. Indian scholarship in the academia of post-colonialism and urban theory, for example, has had major influence on the practice of contemporary art in the recent decades.

WEST HEAVENS is preceded by a series of projects undertaken by the Visual Culture Research Institute. In 2003, as celebration of the 75th anniversary of China Academy of Art, Director Xu Jiang proposed an investigation into the internal boundaries of "Asia", and I was invited to join Gao Shiming and Wu Meichun in the project. Looking at the reality of a parallel system of native and Christian calendars at work within Asian countries, "Asia's Parallel Time" became the theme that coursed through the interdisciplinary investigations and exhibitions that made up "Edges of the Earth: Migration of Contemporary Asian Art and Regional Politics". In 2008, Gao Shiming, Sarat Maharaj, and I co-curated the 3rd Guangzhou Triennial with the project "Farewell to Post-Colonialism", which reviewed the pros and cons of a "East/West" bipolar framework. WEST HEAVENS is a continuation of this work, and it represents an attempt at close encounter between Asian cultures. Professor Kuan-Hsing Chen has committed many years in related academic fields; his participation has honored us and hereby I would like to acknowledge my sincere gratitude to him.

Without his abundant resources in academic circles, this series of forums cannot turn out properly. In additional to this, Chen Yun and Peng Yanhan are the key coordinators in this series of publication. I would also like to thank Michael H. Chen, Sun Tian for their cautious proofing work, Du Keke, Lu Junting, Ye Fuhua, Levis Wang, Zhang Bo, Dai Weijia, Lin Panpan, Zhong Tianya, Xia He, Feng Ying, Cao Yixin, Peng Yanhan and others for their translating work. Thank Heavens Co., Ltd. and Tang Suo for the layout; thank Mr. He Can and Ruan Qingyu from the Nanfang Daily Press; and at last the sponsors Minsheng Art Museum and the Institute.

For more than a century, challenges of imperialism and capitalism have forced India and China to develop political strategies that have profoundly transformed both societies. To share this experience is valuable for Indian and Chinese alike. For China, long before the seismic cultural shift towards the West it had experienced one other profound cultural turn. The Buddhist turn did not come with comparable destructive fervour as the past century of revolutions, but its influence was just as far reaching; Buddhist learning took many centuries before it was fully absorbed into Confucian scholarship. Today, after a century of revolutions, it is important to remember this history of cultural self-transformation. It is critical to remind ourselves that in our imagination of the world there is not just the West, but also the "West Heavens".

序：作为方法的印度

或许是因为过去十年主编 Inter-Asia Cultural Studies: Movement（《亚际文化研究》）国际学刊，与亚洲各地（特别是印度）的批判知识圈产生了工作关系，所以张颂仁与高士明两位先生会找我一起组织将在 2010 年 10 月至 12 月于上海举办的“从西天到中土：印中社会思想对话”的系列活动，由于理念相通，当然就义不容辞地参与了规划工作。他们分派给我的任务之一是替来访的印度学者的读本写序，给了我这个机会说清楚投入这次印中对话的思想背景。

十几年前推动建立《亚际文化研究》学刊的动力，是在有限能力的范围内去改变既有的知识状况，在学术生产的层面上推动亚洲各地的互动与整合。那个时候我们来自亚洲各地十几个地区二十余位的编辑委员，对客观情势进行分析所产生的共识是：总的来说，在整个二十世纪的历史进程中，亚洲各地的知识圈都是把眼睛往欧美看，一个世纪下来，所有事物的基本参照体系都是欧美经验为主。百年之中，这个逐步建立起来、极其稳固的知识结构，造成了学术思想上巨大的问题，不仅是分析视野的窄化，把欧美之外该参照的多元历史经验割除，更糟糕的是欧美的知识方式几乎变成了唯一的典范。但是，历史已经证明这套知识根本无法有效地理解、把握与解释我们自身的生存环境。如何透过亚洲不同次区域之间知识圈的互动，能够彼此看到，进而能使得各地的历史经验成为彼此的参照点，多元转化既有的参照座标，才有可能创造出新的、更具解释力的知识方式。就是凭藉着这个认识论的共识，我们一起走了十年。

回头来看，这条路没有白走。虽然基本格局没有太大的变化，但是上述的知识结构正在被快速地松动当中。过去十年世界情势的变化，正在确立世界是在走向多元并存的时代：拉美地区政权左转、东盟加三的形成、中国与印度的崛起、非洲经济持续成长、奥巴马取代布什政权、欧盟成员的继续增加，等等。相较于1980年代末期，东欧、苏联社会主义阵营的解体，美国强权一枝独秀主宰世界的“全球化”感觉结构，过去十年走向多元政治经济区域的变化，仿佛意味着一元世界的结束。在思想上，原来已经确定、凝固的知识体系，及其所深信不移的价值观，正在快速的崩解当中，以欧美历史经验为基地形成信心十足的解释框架都面临着前所未有的挑战。处于变动的时代，放慢脚步、重新找回世界各地根植于现代历史经验的思想资源，于是成为开创新的知识状况难以跳过的路径。十年很短，《亚际文化研究》还没做出值得彰显的知识方式，但是至少我们已经上路了，尝试着走“亚洲作为方法”的知识路线。

在亚洲，乃至于其他的第三世界地区，既有主流的知识结构之所以会长期以“欧美作为方法”，还是得归咎于世界史的走向，在以欧美为中心向外旋转的力道下，中国也好，印度也罢，都是以“超／赶”（超英赶美）的基本姿势，学习欧美的事物（当然包括了它的价值观），学术思想、知识生产于是被定位成国家民族现代化工程中的主要环节。姑且不要追究“超／赶”的知识方式中暗藏的陷阱，它是否混淆了规范性的目的与客观的历史解释力，至少可以开始问的问题是，一个多世纪下来，现代化的工程到底把原有的这些所谓后发国家变成了什么长相？民主也好，科学也罢，在学习后的搅拌中，实践出了什么新的模样？换句话说，是不是该是停下脚步互相交换一些“超／赶”的经验，在欧美之外的地区之间，互相照照镜子，发现自己从过去变到现在的长相的路径？看清楚了，解释到位了，才能继续走下去，甚至进而发现“超／赶”的知识路线已经走到尽头，该是调整方向的时候了。

如果说知识的目的不是挑空了、为了知识而知识（首先预设了大写真理超越于历史的存在，用来笼罩整个世界），而是为了在世界史的范围内，从多元历史经验的视角，解释各地面对的不同的问题与处境，在相互参照、比较之中，慢慢提炼出具有世界史意义的知识命题，那么，可以说当前所有声称具有普遍主义的理论命题，都不成熟，以欧美经验为参照体系的理论，能够充分解释欧美自身历史就不错了，哪里能够解释其他地区的历史状况，反过来说，对于欧美以外地区的解释必须奠基在其自身历史发展的经验、轨迹当中，不能够简化地、错误地以欧美经验来丈量、解释自身。我想这正是应邀来访的著名的平民研究（Subaltern Studies）历史学家迪佩什·查卡拉巴提（Dipesh Chakrabarty）称之为"将欧洲地方化"（provincializing Europe）的思想方案，或是 2010 年 7 月刚刚过世的沟口雄三教授之所以提出"以中国为方法，以世界为目的"的思想精神之所在。

如果说欧美的历史经验只是一种参照的可能性，特别是它的发展经验与后发地区差距更大，那么在知识转化过程中需要被重新调整的，来访的印度女性主义理论家特贾斯维莉·尼南贾纳（Tejaswini Niranjana）提出的策略，就是必须在欧美之外的地区开展出"替代性的参照框架"（alternative frame of reference），也就是把原来以欧美为参照，多元展开，以亚洲内部、第三世界之间的相互参照，经由参照点的移转，从差异中发展出对于自身历史环境更为贴近的解释。这里思想方案的前提是：关起门来，以本土主义的自闭方式所产生的国粹主义，无法看清楚已经卷入现代的自我，只能沉溺在光辉的过去让自己继续感觉良好而已；打开门来，只以欧美为超赶的参照方式，已然失效，必须在民族国家内部的本土主义（nativism）与欧美中心的世界主义（cosmopolitanism），此两者之外，寻求新的参照体系。

我认为是在上述开启新的知识方式的问题意识下，“作为方法的印度”将会对中国学术思想界产生积极的作用，但是中印之间能够产生对话的前提在于抛弃过去“超／赶”的认识论与知识方式，不能再是以落后／进步、现代化与经济发展的速度等，这些表象来进行比较。用我自己的话来说，就是得先摆脱、搁置规范性的比较，从分析上入手，看清差异，再开始提出内在于历史的解释。

印、中都是世界级的大国，农民占了人口最大的比例，资料显示印度目前是仅次于中国的第二人口大国，将在 2026 年达到 15 亿，超过中国的 13.5 亿成为最大人口国；2015 年印度经济的扩展速度将超过中国。换句话说，抛开其他历史、文化的异同，在社会科学的意义上来说，在世界上所有国家中，对中国最具可比性的就是印度，很难找到其他的地方。

但是，这两个国家也有庞大的差异，印度是多语言、多文化的国家，至今没有统一的语言，国会开会是要经过翻译的，所以很多印度的重要知识分子，如来访的阿希斯 · 南迪（Ashis Nandy），从来就不认为印度是欧洲意义下的民族国家，而是一个文明体。1947 年从殖民地的身份独立，在被大英帝国征服以前，印度地区没有统合的政体，所以独立以后也很难编织出数千年统一的民族历史，必须更为多元复杂地理解它的过去。因为多民族的过去，其中在部分的人口中留下了所谓的种姓制度（caste system），到今天这个社会组织的原则还在运作，政治体制必须要去处理，无法简单地消灭，而是创造机制让底层的人口参与在政治过程当中。由于多语言的社会生存，文化差异与政治运作交叉重叠，不仅形成许多所谓区域性政党，连一些地方性政治人物（如省长），都是以特定语言产生的电影工业中制造出来的明星，以区域性的高知名度，经过普选选出。在此意义上，印度是世界上最大的民主国家，民主运作根植于地方，全国性的政党都必须想办法跟区域性政治力量结合，才能进行有效的统治。

对我个人而言，过去十几年进出印度，每次交流都有问不完的问题，因为南亚经验与东亚实在不同，摆在一起后者的情况变得相对单纯，各个国家地区语言统一，民族国家面貌表面清晰，又不是多元政党，等等。这些有趣的差异，原来该是可以好好研究的，但是我大部分的中国朋友，大陆、香港、台湾都一样，把这些差异在已经习惯使用的"超／赶"的思路逻辑下，做了球赛式的比较：印度太长时间是殖民地，所以中国比较好；印度政治制度是殖民体制的遗留，所以中国比较好，是经过孙中山、毛泽东革命建立起来的（反映的是再次贬低殖民地经验，把战后第三世界主义的世界观丢了）；印度有种姓制度，所以中国比较好，封建制度已经消除（但是并不去追问印度过去的因子是如何与当代社会接轨，反过头来看看自己的社会中是如何与过去衔接，这个社会真是不再封建了吗）；印度是多党的问题，谈的比较少，台湾的人会暂时忘掉欧洲的多党制，把美国两党制搬出来，说只有两党才进步（但是没法儿去问历史问题，印度的多党，乃至于区域政党是为何形成）；还有些人说，印度今天牛还在大城市马路上跑来跑去，哪有中国来得进步，不可以以印度为参照的。总之，如果还是要用简单的"超／赶"逻辑，以欧美树立起来的简单的现代化指标来评比，那就只有等到印度经济超过中国，国力强大的时候，才会进入中国人的视野，现在就继续向天上看吧！

其实，交流必然是双向的，其中会有许多难以避免的错位与误解，举例来说，印度的知识界许多朋友对中国感兴趣，并不是由于它的经济崛起，而是：中国二战后的社会主义阶段与今天经济发展的关系，长远形成的农民文化与政治的关系〔这是以帕沙·查特吉（Partha Chatterjee）为代表的平民研究关切的核心议题〕，社会主义体制与女性解放的问题至今产生了哪些变化，中国如何看待经济发展与资本主义体系之间的关系，中国广大的知识界对于世界的未来有什么不同于欧美的看法，知识界如何在自身的历史实践中提炼出对世界史的解释，等等。总之，以印度为代表的第三世界知识分子，对于中国有基本的尊重，对中国知识界有一定的期待，都与中国社会主义的政治传统有着密切的关系，而与中国是否现代或是进步没有关连，但是，上述这些问题似乎并不是中国知识界感兴趣，或是准备好可以充分对话的。（更让人难过的是，当第三世界地区期待与中国对话时，常常发现中国许多的知识分子对她／他们根本不感兴趣，眼里只有欧美跟自己，还有人跟你说，别搞政治正确了，亚洲根本不存在，第三世界有什么值得对话的。）

我希望已经说清楚了“作为方法的印度”的前提，认识印度是为了去重新认识中国自身与世界，但是也知道当前的知识状况还是处于难以撼动的“超／赶”方式当中，欧美的价值观深入学术思想界，就连是社会主义国度的大陆知识界都很快在赶过港台地区战后“脱亚入欧／美”的知识状况，拥抱欧美知识体系的速度之快，远远超过经济发展，令人惊吓，所以对于这次试图开启的印中对话，我并不抱持很大的希望。

这次活动邀请到的学者，除了杜赞奇（Prasenjit Duara）因为是研究中国历史的专家，很多著作都已经译成中文，其他几位，无论是否生活在印度，他们的知识构成都根植于印度社会与历史，在国际学术界都是非常有分量的学者，年龄上也横跨了三代，从 1937 年出生、1980 年代就早已在国际上赫赫有名的老将阿希斯 · 南迪，到在印度与国际思想界备受尊重、刚刚退休的帕沙 · 查特吉，以及九零年代初以后结构主义翻译理论成名的、壮年一代的文化理论家特贾斯维莉 · 尼南贾纳。读本的翻译工程不小，为的是让中文世界的读者在与他们会面之前或是之后，能够对他们身后的印度社会、历史与文化有更进一步的认识的机会。根据我的理解，这几位重要的思想者大都不是第一次来到中国大陆，对中国有一定程度的认识与想法，我们期待他们的来访，可以让中国的知识界能开始对印度也有相对应的深度认识，成为我们自我转化的契机。

最后，得感谢受邀来访的几位我个人长期的印度友人：女性主义理论家特贾斯维莉·尼南贾纳、社会思想家阿希斯·南迪、平民研究的政治理论家帕沙·查特吉、平民研究的历史学家迪佩什·查卡拉巴提与在中国已经很有名气的历史学家杜赞奇；以及还没缘分会面的著名的艺术理论家萨拉·马哈拉吉（Sarat Maharaj）和在台湾见过一次闻名全球的后殖民理论家霍米·巴巴（Homi Bhabha）教授，感谢他们在百忙中来访，并授予他们著作的翻译出版权。

同时，得特别感谢好友王晓明与王安忆的拔刀相助，以及许江院长与陆兴华两位先生的大力支持，承担起各场与印度学者对话的任务。也谢谢来自香港、台湾及大陆应邀参与不同场次，担任特约讨论人的朋友们。

第一次有机会跟原来素昧平生的张颂仁与高士明两位先生一起工作，感觉很好，有点像是老友重逢一样，我个人很珍惜，他们的心胸、气度与智慧，让我重新发现很多事情只要有心人凑在一起，分工合作，截长补短，都还是有希望的，感谢二位的信任。

陈光兴记于二０一０年八月二十日于新竹交大

India as Method / Kuan-Hsing Chen

It is my great honor to have been asked by Mr. Chang Tsong-Zung and Mr. Gao Shiming to assist in organizing the WEST HEAVENS: INDIA-CHINA SUMMIT ON SOCIAL THOUGHT. They perhaps invited me to participate because in my role as an editor of the journal *Inter-Asia Cultural Studies: Movement* (IACS), over the last ten years I have had a lot of contact with critical thinkers from all over Asia, and particularly those from India. Of course, I was more than happy to take up their invitation, and one of the duties assigned to me was to write an introduction for the READERs introducing the distinguished scholars who will be visiting as part of this event. For me, it is a welcome opportunity to explain the intentions behind this dialogue between India and China.

When we founded *Inter-Asia Cultural Studies: Movement* ten or so years ago, we wanted to make our contribution to changing the condition of knowledge that exists today. We wanted to establish communication and integration among Asian countries, at least within our own circle of academia. The editorial committee was made up of over twenty scholars from every part of Asia, and they were unanimous on one important understanding of our objective history: throughout the 20th century, the gaze of Asian thinkers was fixed on Europe and America. For a hundred years, the basic frame of reference for all knowledge revolved around the Euro-American experience. This framework developed over the course of a century into a highly resilient knowledge structure that created enormous difficulties for Asian thought. It brought about a narrowing of critical perspectives, excluding diverse historical experiences, which should have provided alternative frames of reference. Even more worryingly, Western modes of knowledge became virtually the only paradigm for knowledge. Of course, history has shown that this kind of knowledge is woefully inadequate as we try to comprehend, control and explain the environments in which we exist. At IACS we wanted to generate exchanges between thinkers from each Asian sub-region, make them see each other, turn the historical experience of each region into a potential point of reference for other Asian regions. To create new modes of knowledge and better explanations, we must transform and diversify the frames of reference that contain us. This shared understanding of Asian epistemology has been our guide for more than a decade.

When reviewing the past we would find that our effort has not been in vain. There may not have been a revolution, but the bonds of knowledge structures mentioned above have been loosened considerably. Changes over the last ten years are bringing about a world moving towards diversity. The shift towards the Left in South America, the forming of ASEAN 10+3, the rise of China and India, sustained economic growth in Africa, the handover from Bush to Obama, and the expansion of the EU... At the end of the 1980s, it felt as though "globalization" meant the collapse of Eastern Europe and the Soviet regime, and the unopposed primacy of the United States. But over the past decade the development of multiple political and economic centers seems to have brought an end to the unipolar age. Knowledge systems that were once undeniable and rigid are quickly falling apart, along with their deeply believed values. The highly confident explanatory framework based on the historical experiences of Europe and America faces unprecedented challenges. In this period of transformation, it is time to slow down and take stock, to reconnect with all our intellectual resources rooted in the modern historical experience, to create the pathways we need to new conditions of knowledge. Ten years is very brief. IACS has not yet constructed a mode of knowledge ready for presentation, but we have at least made a start, made an attempt to follow the path of "Asia as method".

In Asia, as in other third world regions, responsibility for the long persistence of "Euro-America as method" must be ascribed to world history. Continually pushed out from the Western centre, China, India and other regions are cast in the permanent role of catch up/overtake (overtaking the UK; struggling to catch up to the US). We learn from Euro-America (including, of course, learning Euro-American values). Academia and the production of knowledge are upheld as the key to the modernization of the nation and its people. Even if we set aside the inherent pitfalls in a knowledge structure predicated on catch up/overtake (does it not conflate normative goals with objective historical explanation?), we must at least start to ask this question: a century on, what exactly has the process of modernization turned these "latecomer" countries into? We learned democracy, we learned science, but what has the application of these concepts brought us? In other words, should we not pause, and take a moment to share our experiences of catch up/overtake? Should non-Western regions not hold up a mirror to each other, uncover the routes they have taken to bring themselves to where they stand today? Moving forward depends on our ability to see, understand and fully explain. In this process, we may even find that the road of catch up/overtake has come to an end, and that it is time to change the direction.

The goal of knowledge is not some kind of unsupported knowledge for its own sake (presupposing a Truth with a capital T which encompasses the whole world and yet lies outside the existence of history). Knowledge is for explaining the problems and situations of each region, within the context of world history, and from a diverse range of historical experience perspectives. Through a process of comparison and cross reference, we gradually distill knowledge propositions which are relevant to world history. None of the theoretical propositions currently held to be universal are mature. Theories grounded in the reference system of the Euro-American experience can at best explain the histories of Europe and America. Expecting them to explain the historical condition of other regions is absurd. On the contrary: explanations in non-Western regions must be in terms of the region's own historical and developmental experience and pathways. One cannot simplistically, improperly apply the Euro-American experience as a measure by which to assess ourselves. I believe this is what visiting subaltern scholar Dipesh Chakrabarty means by his program of "provincialising Europe". It is also very much in the spirit of Professor Mizoguchi Yuzo, who passed away just this July, and his program of "China as method, the world as object".

If the Euro-American historical experience is only one possible reference, and comparing with the development experiences of latecomer countries, there must be a greater gap, then we must seek to transform our knowledge. Tejaswini Niranjana, feminist thinker, has proposed a strategy. She suggests that we create alternative frames of reference for non-Western regions. We move beyond the Euro-American reference frame, and by diversifying it, creating new mutual reference relationships among Asian and third world regions. Through the change of reference, we can use the differences among us to develop better explanations for our own historical environment. Niranjana's program takes it as axiomatic that closing off the region is unproductive; that the closed methods of nativism and nationalism can never clearly perceive the self that has been swept into modernity. All they can manage is to the smug satisfaction of basking in the glow of the past. But even if we are open to other countries, an openness oriented around the catch up/overtake of Euro-American has equally lost its meaning. We must find new reference systems, beyond the ideologies of nativism and cosmopolitanism stuck as they are in the nation-state and in Euro-America.

I believe as China's thinkers become conscious of the problem of developing new modes of knowledge, recognizing India as method will become a productive part of their research. However, a precondition for a dialogue between China and India is that they must both abandon the epistemology and methodology of catch up/overtake. They can no longer seek to compare themselves on measures of how backwards/advanced they are, on modernization, or on pace of economic growth. As I understand it: we must first set aside normative comparisons, and start with analysis. China and India must perceive our differences, then start to suggest explanations immanent in their own history.

India and China are enormous countries on the world scale and farmers make up the bulk of their populations. The latest data suggests that India is at present the second largest country by population, and by 2026 it will have overtaken China, with 1.5 billion people to China's 1.35 billion. In 2015, economic growth rate of India will surpass China's. In other words, if historical and cultural issues are left aside, from a sociological perspective, of all the countries in the world, India is the most comparable to China and no other countries match these two.

But there are enormous differences between the two states. India is a multi-lingual, multi-cultural nation, and it has no official language yet, deliberations in Congress are carried out through interpreters. Many important Indian thinkers, including Ashis Nandy, do not believe that India is a nation-state in the European sense at all. Rather, it is a civilization. In 1947, it freed itself from the identity of the colony. Before being taken over by the British Empire, India was not a united political entity. After independence, it struggled to tell a single national history covering its thousands of years of civilization. It has had to understand its past in a more multiple and complex way. Histories of many Indians groups is the legacy of the caste system, and that social principle still operates today. The political system must deal with this culture. Cultural process cannot simply be eradicated, so instead the polity creates mechanisms by which members of the lower castes can participate in the political process. Because of the many languages, cultural differences intersect with politics. There are local political parties, and some local politicians (such as provincial governors) even win election by virtue of regional fame and pride, having been stars in films in their local dialects. In this sense, India is the world's largest democracy, and the operation of democracy is based in the local. In order to govern effectively, national political parties must find ways to ally with local political forces.

On my own visits to India over the last decade or so, I always have more questions than I have time to ask them. The South Asian experience is very different to the East Asian, and comparing the two, the latter seems more unified because each region of the country has the same language and the surface of nation state is clear, and it does not have a multiple political parties. These interesting differences could be the basis for comparative research. However, most of my Chinese friends, no matter mainland, Hong Kong or Taiwanese, are all stuck in the habit of competitive comparisons via the logic of catch up/overtake: India, they say, was a colony for too long, so China is in a better position (never mind that Taiwan and Hong Kong were colonies, and Chairman Mao once said China is a "semi-colony", not even a whole colony); India's political system is a product of its colonial past, so China's is better, because it was established through the revolutions of Sun Yat-sen and Mao Zedong (again discounting the experience of colonies, and ignoring post-war third cosmopolitanism); India has the caste system, so China is better, having eradicated its feudal systems (but never pursuing how elements of India's past are linked to contemporary society, or looking back to see how their own society connects with the past, and whether it is really no longer feudal); Less frequently it is claimed that India's problem is its multiplicity of political parties, and Taiwanese who raise this point temporarily forget that Europe has many multi-party systems, and try to impose the USA's two party system, claiming that two parties is progress (but without the ability to ask the historical question: how did India's multiple and regional political parties form?); Sometimes I hear that India has cows roaming the streets of its major cities, it's not as advanced as China, we couldn't possibly take India as a reference point. For those determined to apply the simple logic of catch up/overtake, the simple logic of modernization as defined by Euro-America, we will see the economy of India overtake China's, for it to achieve global power status, before it is noticed by the Chinese. Until then, the future will tell!

In fact, communication and exchange must be two-way. And there will be many unavoidable misunderstandings along the way. For example, many of my Indian academic friends are interested in China not because of its economic rise, but for a variety of other reasons: the relationship between China's postwar socialism and its current economic development; the relationship between politics and long-term developments in peasant culture (this is a key concern of research into the working classes, exemplified by the work of Partha Chatterjee); women's liberation and the socialist system, and their interaction; how China understands the relationship between economic development and capitalist systems; what new, non-Western viewpoints China's greatly expanded academia will bring to the world; how China's scholars distil explanations of world history from their own historical practice. Third world scholars have a basic respect for China, and have certain expectations of Chinese thinkers. Both respect and expectation are very much connected to China's socialist political tradition; they are not a function of whether China has advanced, or whether it has achieved modernity. However, these issues are not the ones interest in Chinese thinkers, nor ones on which they are prepared to carry out a dialogue. (Even more frustratingly, as the third world looks forward to establishing a dialogue with China, it often finds that China's thinkers do not return the compliment. For the Chinese thinker, there is only Euro-American and China. They tell me: Don't play at political correctness! Asia does not exist, what value can there be in a dialogue with the third world.)

I hope that I have made clear the motivation behind "India as Method". Understanding India is a way to understand afresh oneself, China itself and the world. But our current condition of knowledge is enmeshed in a method of catch up/overtake that is difficult to escape. Euro-American values permeate academia. Even in socialist mainland China, intellectuals are following and even outdoing postwar Taiwan and Hong Kong in their eagerness to "escape Asia, join Euro-America". The speed at which Chinese thought is embracing Euro-American knowledge systems is shocking, far faster than our economic growth. So I do not hold out great hopes for this attempt to start a dialogue between China and India. All I can hope for is that those friends who want to find another avenue for understanding can begin to perceive India, in preparation for future exchanges.

The invited scholars, Prasenjit Duara is already familiar to many, because the history of China is his field of study, many of his works have been translated into Chinese, and the other scholars, whether currently residing in India or not, their structures of knowledge that are rooted in Indian society and history. They represent three generations of Indian scholarship: Ashis Nandy, born in 1937, is already a scholar of global renown in the 1980s; Partha Chatterjee, just retired, widely respected in India and internationally; while cultural theorist Tejaswini Niranjana is in the prime of her career, having made major contributions to post-structural translation theory in the 1990s. The translation of this READERs has been a major undertaking. We are aiming for giving readers in the World of Chinese an opportunity to understand the Indian society, history and culture in which these thinkers. According to my understanding, this is not the first time any of these scholars has visited mainland of China. Each of them has a level of understanding and insight into China. We hope that their visit will give Chinese academia the beginning of an equally deep knowledge of India. It will be an opportunity for us to practice the self-transformation.

Finally, I must thank personal friends for agreeing to participate: feminist theorist Tejaswini Niranjana; social thinker Ashis Nandy; working class historian and political theorist Partha Chatterjee; working class historian Dipesh Chakrabarty; and historian Duara Prasenjit who is already so well-known in China; the art theorist Sarat Maharaj, whom I have not had the pleasure to meet; and world-famous postcolonial theorist Professor Homi K. Bhabha, whom I met on one occasion in Taiwan. Appreciate them for making time to come to China, and for granting us translation rights for the essays presented in these READERs.

I'd also like to give special thanks for the ready assistance offered by my friends Wang Xiaoming and Wang Anyi, and for the support of President Xu Jiang and professor Lu Xinghua, they have been responsible for organizing the dialogues with our visiting scholars. Thanks also to friends from Hong Kong, Taiwan and the mainland who have agreed to be interlocutors for the discussion sessions.

This has been my first opportunity to work with Chang Tsong-Zung and Gao Shiming, and it has been a great pleasure. From them, I have been lucky enough to find alike minds with a common goal, and I have treasured the opportunity. Their boldness, openness and wisdom have reminded me that so long as we can come together and pool our contributions, there's always a hope.

August 20, 2010, Chiao Tung University, Hsinchu

迪佩什 · 查卡拉巴提
Dipesh Chakrabarty

迪佩什 · 查卡拉巴提 (Dipesh Chakrabarty) 拥有澳大利亚国立大学历史学博士学位，印度管理学院管理学研究生文凭（相当于 MBA），以及加尔各答大学总统学院理学学士（荣誉）学位。

他现在在芝加哥大学历史及南亚语言文明专业任教，被当选为罗伦斯 · A · 金普顿杰出贡献教授，他也是芝加哥当代理论中心的研究员，英语系的助理研究员，澳大利亚国立大学人文研究院访问学者，澳大利亚墨尔本大学历史研究院荣誉教授教职。

2004 年，查卡拉巴提当选美国艺术与科学研究院会员，又于 2006 年当选澳大利亚人文学院荣誉会员。2007 年，他在国际研究联合会大会上被颁发“杰出学者奖”。伦敦大学也于 2010 年 9 月为他颁发文学硕士（荣誉）学位。

查卡拉巴提是贱民研究的开山祖师之一，也是《评论探索》杂志的两位编辑之一，以及《后殖民研究》杂志的第一位编辑。他是《公共文化》杂志的编辑，《历史罗盘》杂志的董事会成员，也担任《美国历史评论》杂志的编委会成员。他和哥伦比亚大学的谢尔顿 · 保洛克（Sheldon Pollock）以及加州大学洛杉矶校区的三桔 · 萨布拉曼洋（Sanjay Subrahmanyam）是《跨学科南亚研究》（由芝加哥大学、哥伦比亚大学以及加州大学三家联合出版）系列的编辑。查卡拉巴提也是柏林洪堡论坛专家委员会成员。

查卡拉巴提是柏林科学研究所的成员（2008-2009 年），维也纳人类研究所学者，华盛顿大学卡茨教授（2009 年）；曼切斯特大学霍兹华兹访问教授（2010 年），Iowa 大学杰出访问教授（2002 年）；明尼苏达大学高等研究所杰出访问学者（2007 年）；立陶宛维尔纽斯欧盟人文大学访问教授（2006 年）；纽约普拉特研究院常驻学者（2005 年）；悉尼大学访问研究学者（2005 及 2009 年）；尼赫鲁大学历史研究中心访问学者（2005 年）；纽约州立大学人文中心（2004 年）；加尔各答社会科学研究中心（2003 年）；普林斯顿人文研究院访问学者（2002 年）；加州大学伯克莱分校历史系访问副教授。此外还参与了在澳大利亚、印度以及美国其他地方的研究项目。

查卡拉巴提正在撰写两本书，将于近期完成并且由芝加哥大学出版社出版。书名分别是：《不合时宜的历史学家：欧洲以及印度历史研究的开始》《历史的气候：论文集（4 篇）》。他的一些德语文章目前正由柏林的校园出版社出版，还有一些孟加拉语的文章由 Ananda 出版社出版。他的其他论著包括：《工人阶级历史之思考：孟加拉 1890 - 1940》（普林斯顿出版社，1989 年，2000 年）；《地方化欧洲：后殖民思想以及历史差异》（普林斯顿，2000 年，第二版，2007 年）；《现代性的居所：贱民研究文集》（芝加哥大学出版社，2000 年）。他还编辑了《贱民研究》第 9 卷（德里，牛津大学出版社，1996 年）（与 Shahid Amin 一道）；《大都市主义》（杜克大学出版社，2000 年）（其他几位编辑是 Carol Breckenridge, Homi Bhabha 和 Sheldon Pollock）；《从殖民到后殖民：转型中的印度和巴基斯坦》（德里，牛津大学出版社，2007 年）（其他两位编辑是 Rochona Majumdar 和 Andrew Sartori）；《历史的公共生活》（《公共文化》专刊，2008 年，其他作者包括 Bain Attwood 和 Claudio Lomnitz）。《地方化欧洲》已经被翻译为意大利语、西班牙语和法语，而且土耳其语、波兰语以及朝鲜语的版本正在翻译。《现代性的居所》正在被翻译为阿拉伯语。另有两篇文章于 2009 年被翻译为西班牙语出版：《全球化之下的人文主义》以及《非殖民化和文化政策》。

DIPESH CHAKRABARTY holds a B.Sc (Hons.) degree from Presidency College, University of Calcutta, a Post-graduate Diploma in Management (considered equivalent to MBA) from the Indian Institute of Management, Calcutta, and a Ph.D (History) from the Australian National University.

He is currently the Lawrence A. Kimpton Distinguished Service Professor in History, South Asian Languages and Civilizations, and the College at the University of Chicago. He is also a Faculty Fellow of the Chicago Center for Contemporary Theory, an Associate Faculty of the Department of English, holds a visiting position at the Research School of Humanities at the Australian National University, and is an Honorary Professorial Fellowship with the School of Historical Studies at the University of Melbourne, Australia .

Chakrabarty was elected Fellow of the American Academy of Arts & Sciences in 2004 and Honorary Fellow of the Australian Academy of the Humanities in 2006. He was awarded an "Eminent Scholar Award" at the International Studies Association Convention in 2007. The University of London has invited him to receive the degree of D. Litt (Honoris causa) in September 2010 .

Chakrabarty is a founding member of the editorial collective of Subaltern Studies, a co-editor of *Critical Inquiry*, and a founding editor of

Postcolonial Studies. He is a Contributing Editor to *Public Culture*, a member of the Board for *History Compass* and has served on the editorial boards of the *American Historical Review*. He is one of the editors (along with Sheldon Pollock from Columbia University and Sanjay Subrahmanyam from UCLA) of the new series *South Asia Across the Disciplines* published by a consortium of three university presses (Chicago, Columbia, and California). He also serves on the Board of Experts for the Humboldt Forum in Berlin.

He has been, by invitation, a Fellow at the Wissenschaftskolleg zu Berlin (2008-09): Institut für die Wissenschaften von Menschen, Vienna (2010); Katz Professor in the Humanities, University of Washington, Seattle (2009); Hallsworth Visiting Professor, The University of Manchester, U.K. (2010); Ida Beam Distinguished Visiting Professor at the University of Iowa (2007); Distinguished Visitor, Institute of Advanced Study, The University of Minnesota (2007); Visiting Professor, European Union Humanities University, Vilnius, Lithuania (2006), Scholar-in-Residence, Pratt Institute, New York (2005); Visiting Fellow, Max Planck Institute for Historical Sciences, Goettingen (2005); Faculty, Seminar in Experimental Critical Theory, University of California, Irvine (2005); Visiting Research Professor, University of Technology, Sydney (2005 and 2009); Visitor, Center for Historical Studies, Jawaharlal Nehru University, Delhi (2005); Visitor, Humanities Center, State University of New York, Stony Brook (2004);

Hitesranjan Sanyal Visiting Professor of History, Centre for Studies in Social Sciences, Calcutta (2003); Visiting Fellow, Humanities Institute, Princeton (2002); Visiting Assistant Professor, Department of History, University of California, Berkeley, and has held other fellowships in Australia, India, and the US.

Chakrabarty is currently engaged in completing two books to be published by the University of Chicago Press. They are provisionally entitled *The Untimely Historian: Europe and the Birth of Historical Research in India* and *The Climate of History: Four Theses*. A collection of his essays in German in being brought out by Campus Verlag in Berlin and a collection in Bengali by Ananda Publishers. His other publications include: *Rethinking Working-Class History: Bengal 1890-1940* (Princeton: 1989, 2000); *Provincializing Europe: Postcolonial Thought and Historical Difference* (Princeton, 2000; second edn. 2007); *Habitations of Modernity: Essays in the Wake of Subaltern Studies* (Chicago, 2000); He has also edited (with Shahid Amin) *Subaltern Studies IX* (Delhi: OUP, 1996), (with Carol Breckenridge, Homi Bhabha, and Sheldon Pollock) *Cosmopolitanism* (Duke, 2000); (with Rochona Majumdar and Andrew Sartori) *From the Colonial to the Postcolonial: India and Pakistan in Transition* (Delhi: OUP, 2007); (with Bain Attwood and Claudio Lomnitz) "The Public Life of History," a special issue of *Public Culture* (2008). *Provincializing Europe* has been translated into Italian, Spanish and French, and is being brought out in Turkish, Polish, and Korean. *Habitations* is being translated into Arabic. A collection of two essays translated into Spanish was published in 2009: *El humanismo en la era de la globalizacion* and *La descolonizacion y las politicas culturales* (Buenos Aires: Katz Editores, and Barcelona: Centro de Cultura Contemporanea de Barcelona, 2009).

目录
CONTENTS

作为机遇的滞后：
庶民历史再研究

一

即便我在这篇文章里讨论的是史学而不是艺术，我不得不承认这篇文章的标题源于克里斯托弗 · 平尼教授一次偶然的邀请。平尼教授是著名的南亚视觉文化史学家，他于 2008 年 5 月在芝加哥的西北大学举办了一场艺术史大会，并邀请我在大会上发言。在这次大会上受邀发表演讲，使我想起自己最近一次接触到有“滞后”这个主题还是在 2007 年芝加哥举办的一个印度艺术展上。

那年，一个名叫“来自印度的当代艺术”的精彩展览在芝加哥文化中心展出。古拉默罕默德 · 谢赫、娜莉妮 · 马拉尼、苏博德 · 古普塔、维万 · 孙达拉姆等艺术大家的艺术作品令人印象深刻。但名为《新叙事：来自印度的当代艺术》的展览目录，清楚地指出为“新”和“当代”之类的词语背书（underwrite）的时间感是什么。[1] 正如该展览策展人贝蒂 · 赛德在卷首语里所言，印度艺术也是可以是一种“当代”艺术，因为它反映出印度在新千年里被认可为世界主要大国的一种姿态。美国的博物馆一直不愿购买或展出印度的当代艺术品，因为美国人认为，那时印度的当代艺术家还是“停留在一种狭隘的、自我对比的民族志研究模式中”，而没有达到“真正从在印度的生活和工作中汲取真谛”的状态。[2] 时至今日，很多西方的当代艺术策展人对印度当代艺术开始重视起来，原因很明显：印度的当代艺术家已经迎头赶上世界当代艺术的浪潮了。

我在想，“滞后魔咒”是否已经在印度破除了？这本展览目录这样介绍现代主义和女性主义艺术在印度的历史："和现代主义一样，女性主义艺术传到印度要比传到西方要晚"。[3]印度艺术在被西方世界确认为"当代"以前，不会成为"全球的"或"世界的"——"当代性"似乎早为西方世界所获取，至少早于印度艺术多年。"电子时代的通讯能力为我们提供了关于艺术生产的全球性认知，许多20世纪中期的印度艺术家无法获得这一点，"画册的文字这样解释，并继续道：

在1947年印度独立之前，西方现代艺术在印度可以说是无人知晓。印度艺术家没有接触到现代艺术史的逐步演进。相反，现代艺术史通过印度当地的展览和新近开始有的到国外游学的机会，一股脑儿地席卷了印度艺术家[4]。

我对平尼教授的邀请深感荣幸，但对我来说，这在形式和个人的层面亦牵涉了"滞后"的问题。他们选我做嘉宾是那次大会一个"滞后的决定"，原因是那次大会的第二位主要演讲者就在大会开始前最后一刻说不能来，我于是被紧急安排到会场去救场。我感觉我所处的情况有些像后来印度全国广播电台所说的"为节目单中的艺人救场"。我受到很友好但滞后的邀请——但这不是任何人的错；可这就是这个事情如何得到解决的经过。此外，平尼教授传阅的大会总结陈词中所隐约预示的一些主题也牵涉"滞后"的理念。本届大会本来是预期成为"特定史学逻辑"的窗口。

一些特定的艺术生产模式，因为被看作是“滞后”的而被取消了进入艺术史“正典”（canon）的资格——我猜印度的现代主义就是这样一个例子。“只有一种时间性（temporality）利害攸关？”总结陈词发出这样的疑问。事实上，总结陈词正是出于对这样的判断的一种反叛才提出来的：“白色立方体据说是具有普世化作用的空间本身仅仅是一种欧美幻想……？一种全球性的做法会不会要求一种躲避‘全球性’之可能性的异质性？……可不可以用‘流动’来取代‘地域’？”而且它也正面回应了评判的问题：“在不熟悉的审美世界中，价值的归属是如何可能的？……这种归属对一种世界性艺术（a World Art）来说是不是必要的？”[5]

所以在答应了“滞后”地在大会上作有关“滞后”的发言时，我想起流传在我家乡加尔各答的一则笑话。在加尔各答上了年纪的孟加拉人都会有个习惯，他们喜欢在人名后边加上“达”来表示对这个人的尊重。比如他们称阿希斯·南迪为“阿希斯达”，罗纳吉·古哈为“罗纳吉达”。当哲学家德里达在加尔各答为一个书展揭幕并发言的时候，很多不了解外国做派的人会想当然地以为德里达可能是原名为“德里”的孟加拉老头，凑巧的是“德里”在孟加拉语里是“滞后”的意思，而出于对其的尊敬，才称呼他“德里达”。所以当我在大会上仅仅是顶替未能到场的人时，这一连串有关这位著名哲学家的联想使我对我将在本文中阐述的思想之一——“滞后与替代（displacement）之间的关系”，因为我觉得正是这种关系使得滞后有可能转化成机会或者“可能性”，而这也是我在本文的题目中暗示的一层联系。

平尼教授在大会总结陈词中所提出的那些问题，一直回响在作为历史学家的我的工作过程中常常光顾的庶民历史（subaltern histories）的殿堂之中。其实在《庶民研究》中，“滞后”的主题以及某种反叛“滞后”的精神比比皆是。那个讨论是《庶民研究》，我们曾经只构想为印度的项目的系列丛书，最终成为全球 / 世界历史之一部分的过程中关键的部分。所以，虽然平尼教授的大会给世界艺术这个表达的“世界”加上了括号，请让我来讨论一下，当我们把“滞后”转化为可能性时，那被构建而成的世界。读者也会看到，当“滞后”的套路用在艺术史学中从而引发的评判问题，同样也出现在政治史学中：在庶民历史成为一个新兴的全球构造的时候，我们如何评估庶民历史中的进展?

二

《庶民研究》自诞生之日起就被一些评论家说成是一个“滞后的”项目，在南亚次大陆上做英国所谓“自下而上的历史”很久以前成就的东西。在持这种观点的评论家中，比较出名的一位是阿里夫 · 德里克（Arif Dirlik）。事实上，历史研究中的滞后已经不是新问题了，哈佛大学著名历史学家亚历山大 · 格申克伦（Alexander Gerschenkron）在二十世纪六十年代早期就已经在他的著作《从历史视角看经济落后》中提到过了。在该书中，格申克伦透过“滞后”和“赶上”更“现代”的国家的政治之棱镜对俄国现代化进程问题做了剖析。[6] 印度首相尼赫鲁在印度独立后常说，印度要用几十年的时间走完美国人几百年的路。正如我在《地方化欧洲》（*Provincializing Europe*）中所试图论证的，“滞后”是十九世纪产生的某种历史主义的世界观不可或缺的一部分。我从去年芝加哥的展览目录中摘引的词句将会表明，此种世界观仍然在影响公共领域中的艺术史讨论。

“滞后”的问题指向历史的重复和再认知的问题。如果在一个由前后关系概念构架的场域中，发生了一件同另一件事相似的事情，那么后发生的这件事情即被视为“滞后”。这反过来提出了一个霍米·巴巴（Homi Bhabha）借用拉什迪（Salman Rushdie）的话颇有些紧迫感地问过的问题：新事物是如何进入这个世界的？[7] 我们如何在看来不过是重复的东西之中觉察到新的东西?

我想在这里向读者提出两个可能看来有些矛盾的命题。我的第一个命题是：任何新事物总是通过替代旧事物来到这个世界上的；我的第二个命题是：新事物往往会扰乱人们的判断，因为在我们看来很多新事物仅仅是重复从而是不足的。 新事物常常很难同既非拷贝又非原作的仿像（simulacrum）相区别。对新事物开放，即意味着进行一场海德格尔式的斗争：聆听我尚未理解的东西。判断，我这里指政治判断，使这成为一个非常困难的任务。在本文剩下的篇幅中，我将以《庶民研究》为例详细阐释我的命题。

在我展开讨论之前，我有必要在这里引用一下吉尔·德勒兹（Gilles Deleuze）的理论，我们时代的思想家中，他对这些问题比谁思考的都多。他首先区分了“重复”与“共性”，以便进而区分“重复”与“相似”。德勒兹说：“‘重复’不是‘共性’，而‘重复’与‘相似’也是两码事”。在德勒兹看来，“共性”呈现两个主要的秩序：相似的质的秩序，以及对等的量的秩序。循环以及均等是二者各自的象征。而另一方面，“重复”指的是不可置换与不可替代的唯一性。重复“是以一种特定的方式行事，但相对于某种独一无二或具有唯一性的东西。”[8]

如果说置换是共性的判断标准，那么“偷窃”和“赠予”就是重复的判断标准……这是各色节庆显而易见的矛盾：它们重复着不可能重复的东西，它们没有为第一次加上第二或第三次，而是为第一次带上了n次幂。不是说联盟节（*Fête de la Fédération*）纪念和代表了攻占巴士底狱，而是攻占巴士底狱是对联盟节的庆祝，并预先重复了所有后来的联盟节，或者说莫奈的第一幅睡莲重复了所有其他的。因而共性，作为特殊的共相，对立于作为唯一物的普遍性的重复。一件艺术品的重复如同一个无概念的唯一性，诗歌必须能熟读成诵也并不是偶然的。[9]

这段话中所暗示的法律与诗、历史与记忆之间的区别，赋予了重复越界的力量。重复的戏剧和替代的戏剧相对，正如运动同概念、同将其指回概念的再现，都是相对的。[10]德勒兹明确表示："重复"乃是新事物进入世界的方式，但通过的是利用伪装和替代的手段——"伪装和替代一样都形成了重复的一部分"——因为重复(这是德勒兹对克尔凯郭尔和尼采的解读）是"习惯和记忆的双重定罪"，而我们将会看到，习惯和记忆正是政治判断的基础。[11]这样，"重复"构建了政治判断的一个危机。

三

现在我将通过《庶民研究》的例子为诸位详尽阐释德勒兹式"重复"的两个方面，即替代与伪装。首先，我将用文献资料梳理替代这一主题，随后再转向"伪装"这个更加复杂的主题。

我是从1982年开始介入《庶民研究》这个书系的，该书系是以政治为驱动力的史学的一个例证。因为政治观判断对这个项目至关重要。它肇端于南亚马克思主义历史写作传统，其最初的指导思想的表述成型受益于毛泽东与安东尼奥·葛兰西（Antonio Gramsci）。印度的左翼的历史写作传统受到了（也许不太出人意料）英国马克思主义或社会主义史学"自下而上"的传统的深刻影响。爱德华·汤普森（Edward Thompson）、埃里克·霍布斯鲍姆(Eric Hobsbawm)、克里斯托弗·希尔(Christopher Hill)和乔治·鲁迪（George Rudé）等人是这一传统筚路蓝缕的开派宗师。正如汤普森所写的英国人民史取决于"下层人民在英国民主历史中有何贡献？"这一问题一样，《庶民研究》书系的历史学家也以一个相似的问题开场：庶民阶层在印度国族主义政治的历史中有何贡献？进而对印度的民主政体有何贡献？[12]但相似点到此为止。英国马克思主义大众史学叙述基于一种发展的时间观：在这个叙事中，农民阶层要么消亡，要么被取代从而产生出工人阶级；工人阶级通过捣毁机器运动、宪章运动和其他权利斗争，某一天蜕变成为公民和无产阶级革命者。第三世界的农民以及部族——时空仿佛穿越了数百年——突然一下子面对抛在他们眼前的殖民地国家及其现代官僚和压迫机器，在这种思维模式中被看作是“前政治的”个人。他们虽然不得不对付现代的统治机制，可是他们不理解这些统治机制的运作语言。就英国的“自下而上”的提议而言，只有经年累月，通过一个心智发展的历程，庶民阶层才能转化为一种现代政治力量。

《庶民研究》首先摒弃此种“成为政治的（个体）”的发展观。它宣称：农民和庶民阶层自反抗殖民当局统治的那一刻起就是**政治的**。[13]说他们的行动是“政治的”，是因为他们对殖民管治的体制基础——殖民政府，以及地主和高利贷者——作出了回应并产生了影响。我们平常没有过多地考虑庶民（the subaltern）可以不需要经由一种“政治发展”的过程就成为“政治的”这一主张所隐含的意义。但在我们的史学中，这一主张的涵义依然是非常显要的。

这里我觉得有必要阐释，帝国主义和反殖民主义的历史遗产在这个潜在的辩论〔即庶民是否经过一段时间（通过某种训导）才变得具有政治性，抑或庶民阶层可能本身就具有政治素养的天性？〕之中互有交流。发展的时间（developmental time），或者说那种阶段论（stadial）史观的时间观基础，可以说是帝国主义统治对印度的馈赠。这即为“未然”的时间，我在《地方化欧洲》中这样称呼它。像穆勒（John Stuart Mill）（甚或马克思）这样的欧洲政治家在思考历史时会运用到这样的时间结构。另一方面，民族主义者以及反殖民主义者在二十世纪摈弃这种对时间的想象，要求立刻被给予自治，不容许有等待或准备，不容许有延迟——“当下”。取代了他们想象当中这种“未然”的结构的是“当下”的视角。[14]

十九世纪的时候，英国政府反对给予受过良好教育的印度人自治权，并给出了如下理由：这些印度人并不能代表更广泛的印度“人民”。

对此的回应来自甘地。在一战期间进入印度政坛之后，他将主要的民族主义政党，印度国民大会党，转变成了一个“群众”组织。他通过将农民当作普通的、所谓“四安那”（4-anna 为印度辅币，相当于四分之一卢比）的具有党内投票权的成员来获取他们的支持。国大党的“群众基础”使其领导人能够宣称自己是“代表”整个国家，即使在英印当局统治下的穷人和文盲不具备任何正式选举权。在此种代表观念中，分割农民和受过教育的领袖的那条教育的鸿沟从来不被认为是个问题。因为人们假定，农民完全有能力做出被殖民统治所剥夺的那些公民选择。二十世纪二十年代初开始，甘地便倡导在未来独立的印度给予成年人普选权。这样，印度的农民在印度独立一夜之间就被塑造为公民（至少在投票方面如此），而不需要历经正式或非正式教育所需要的发展性时间——这就是民族主义者所要求的“当下”。在印度独立后的立宪大会上的制宪辩论中，后来成为政治家的哲学家萨瓦帕利·拉达克里希南博士（Dr. Sarvepalli Radhakrishnan）主张一个具有共和形式的政体，他宣称几千年的文明的浸染——即使正式的教育是阙如的——已经使印度农民为这样一个国家作好了准备。[15]

为这种对群众的现代政治能力的带有反殖民主义和民粹主义色彩的信仰，是由另一个欧洲传统、某种历史诗学（poetics of history）背书的。这种传统就是浪漫主义。的确，涵盖农民和工人的反殖民运动的中产阶级领袖们不曾抛弃发展的时间观以及对农民的教育和训导方略。甘地以及其他民族主义领袖的著作常常表达出对无法无天的暴民的恐惧，把教育看作是这一问题的解决之道。[16] 但这种恐惧被其对立面——这种对于群众的政治信仰——所中和。在二十世纪二十和三十年代，此种浪漫主义给印度民族主义打上了烙印—— 比如很多不属于共产党或者左派的民族主义者都会表露出这种信仰。从事印地语文学研究的弗兰切斯卡·奥斯尼（Francesca Orsini）最近挖掘出记录这种倾向的一系列证据。从她的选文中随手拈来一些例子，比如印地文报纸《普拉塔普》（*Pratap*）的主编加内什·申卡·维迪雅迪（Ganesh Shankar Vidyarthi）在1915年5月31日发表的社论：

在印度那些受尽鄙视的农民其实是我们的衣食父母，而不是那些自命不凡、把不得不生活在劳作和贫穷之中的人看作是贱种的人们。[17]

维迪雅迪在1915年1月11日的社论中也曾谈到：

是时候让我们的政治意识形态和我们的运动不被局限在受过英式教育的人群当中，向广大普通人扩散了。是时候让印度的公共舆论不被那极少数受过教育的人的看法所局限，而要反映全国各阶层的人民的思想了。民主治国就是公共舆论治国。[18]

人们应该意识到，这种对群众的浪漫主义——政治信仰也是传统意义上的民粹主义信仰。正如十九世纪末的俄国民粹主义，这种思想模式不仅在农民中寻求一种“好的”政治素质，而且通过这一步骤，能把农民这种所谓的“落后”转化为历史优势。那些没有被资产阶级自我中心的个人主义所腐化的农民阶层，被想象为已被赋予开启一种和西方盛行的所不同的、更社群主义的现代性的能力。[19]殖民统治下极为有限的选举权同农民和城市贫民同时被引入民族主义运动这二者之间所蕴含的矛盾有一个非常重要的后果。加在宪政上的限制，意味着田间地头、工厂、巴扎、集市，甚至普通的街巷都成为了独立自治斗争的主战场。正式在这些战场上，庶民主体以他们惯有的集体动员模式（当然也包括公众暴力的做法）进入了公共生活。

因而，印度群众政治时代的开启，是由展现民粹思想的关键全球特征的意识形态促成的。首先，存在一种倾向，在农民或群众中看到某种政治上的美德。此外还存在一种倾向，将殖民判断认为是滞后和劣势的东西看成是历史优势。在“落后”中看到“优势”——亦即将滞后看作是一种机遇——也是对阶段论史观假设的时间概念的挑战。这是把殖民地的“未然”时态扭转为民主和反殖民的“现在”结构。

给出这样一个压缩的印度民主思想（但不是印度民主政体的，这一区别很重要）的浪漫—民粹渊源历史，是为了提出对我的阐述来说很关键的一个论点。在《庶民研究》（1982 年创刊）的早期期刊中以及拉纳吉特 · 古哈（Ranajit Guha）《殖民时期印度的农民起义的基本方面》都坚持：农民或庶民阶层其实一直都是“政治的”，而不是发展时间观意义上的“前政治时期的”。此种坚持在某种程度上可以说是对英属印度反殖民群众运动中所隐含的民粹主义前提的重述。[20] 但就对我个人来说，这其中还有对民粹主义这个词的“替代”成分。《庶民研究》中的民粹主义更强烈也更明显。首先，《庶民研究》的分析之中没有“对群众的恐惧”。

也没有任何对结社或政党的需要的探讨（这一点有违经典马克思主义或列宁主义的分析）。古哈以及他的同仁都在毛泽东的著作（特别是毛泽东 1927 年关于湖南农民运动的报告）以及葛兰西的《狱中札记》里得到灵感和启发。然而，他们对毛泽东以及葛兰西的利用说明了《庶民研究》诞生的时代背景。这毕竟是 1970 年代：一个被阿尔都塞等人所尊崇的全球毛主义的年代。1971 年，葛兰西札记的一些节选开始陆续有英文版问世。在 1968 年捷克斯洛伐克遭到苏联入侵后，人们把毛泽东和葛兰西视为跳出斯大林主义或苏联马克思主义的通途。《庶民研究》的不少历史学者都是 1969 到 1971 年之间在印度部分地区爆发的毛主义运动的参与者或同情者。[21]

然而，不管是毛泽东所倡导的“抓住党的领导权”的理论抑或是葛兰西的抑制 “自发性”的理论都不是我们写作的重点。古哈在他的《殖民主义时期印度的农民起义的基本方面》一书中牢牢抓住在十九世纪英国统治下的印度（即在甘地的大众民族主义出现前）起义农民如何动员起来的主线来理解。通过对构成反抗（因而对古哈来说也是一个庶民的政治领域）的动员、沟通和公共暴力等创造空间和时间的实践进行结构主义的分析，古哈寻求把农民作为这些暴动的集体作者来理解。从古哈的社会主义观点看来，农民自己单干所能取得的成果是有限的，不过这种局限性并不要求党派作为媒介。对反抗的崇拜标志着《庶民研究》的早期努力，令人想起毛泽东在文化大革命期间的一句名言:“造反有理”。的确,从一个全球的角度来看,我们可以说《庶民研究》是漫长的左翼全球史的最后,或者说最新的一个例子。这种浪漫主义的民粹主义塑造了二十世纪的毛主义的主要部分,同时也在葛兰西将正当看作现代版的君主的思想中所有的二律背反和模棱两可中留下深深的烙印。

因此,在西方工业社会外寻找革命主体已经有很长的历史,从十九世纪晚期的俄国到殖民地和半殖民地(毛主义的词汇)的第三世界,这曾是一种全球性的寻找,也是一种本身具有浪漫主义的寻找。此种浪漫主义的政治潜能到今天已经被耗尽。但当我们回望的时候,我们还是能看到在工业化程度相对较低的国家寻找革命主体的历史中困难重重的原因。这样的一个革命主体本身不可能是无产者。我们很难去定义一个世界历史意义上的革命主体,该主体将取代那些在渐渐地被吸纳入资本主义的引力圈的农民基础的经济体中未曾存在(无论如何未曾大量存在)的工业劳工阶级。革命会成为托洛茨基所说的取代主义的行径吗?政党会取代工人阶级吗?在政党领导下的农民会成为一个革命的阶级吗?它会成为庶民范畴还是弗朗茨·法农(Frantz Fanon)所谓的“世上苦难的人”?

当年轻的“左派黑格尔”马克思设想出无产阶级这一范畴作为终将取代资产阶级的新革命主体时——这还是在恩格斯完成他

1844年有关曼彻斯特工人阶级的著作之前——这一范畴具有哲学上的精确性。这种理论似乎也在因工业革命而诞生的工人阶级中找到了社会学上的对应。但诸如毛泽东所说的“农民”、葛兰西所说的“庶民”、法农所说的“世界上苦难的人”，还有列宁和卢卡奇所说的“作为革命主体的政党”之类的名目并不具备哲学或社会学上的精确性。好像对非无产者的革命主体（在缺乏大的工人阶级的情况下）的追寻，就是对原先的术语——无产阶级——的一系列替换练习。法农本身就是一个生动的例子。他的传记作家大卫·马赛（David Macey）指出，法农的那句名言“世界上苦难的人”影射《国际歌》的歌词“起来，全世界受苦的人”，此处指的就是无产阶级。但法农用这句话指涉另外的一样东西，而非无产阶级。法农自己也无法确知他指的到底是什么，但他可以肯定的是，在殖民地它不可能是无产者。人们只需要记得法农在其著作的开首就警告道：“马克思主义分析在我们需要处理殖民问题时总应该被稍微延展。”[22]

一个没有恰当名分的集体主体，一个只能由对原本的欧洲字眼“无产阶级”的一系列的替换而命名的主体——这既是一种失败也是一种新的开始的条件。失败是显而易见的。它在于缺乏特定性或定义。新开始又在哪里？首先，这种不精确本身指向了全球性的对世界的社会主义转化的努力的语境中，欧洲中心主义的思想的缺陷所在。在工业化国家之外，革命主体甚至没有得到理论上的定义。这种偏差的历史等同于一种承认：如果我们想通过欧洲发明的字眼去理解全球大众政治行为的本质，我们只是在求助于一系列的替代品罢了（而且我们还无暇理会那些词语本身是否就是幻像）。何以言之？因为尽管我们承认我们都是处在十九世纪欧洲浪漫主义革命思潮的荫蔽之下，我们还是在欧洲政治思想的局限之中讨生活。意识到诸如“大众”、“庶民”以及“农民”这些词的替代性本质之后，我建议第一步应该写通过反殖民的民族主义而出现的大众政治民主历史，因为在这里边必定含有群体主体。可是这种写作方法只能在有意识地穿越欧洲思想的局限时才能被理解。如果直接去寻找革命的世界性的历史主体，必定只能碰到替代物。在全球范围内对非无产阶级的革命主体进行概括的尝试失败后，人们开始尝试在西方世界以外寻找新思想与研究，这样一来便出现很多替代包括“无产阶级”在内的欧洲政治范畴。

综上所述，由于历史学家孜孜不倦地为很多社会主义政治的思想在欧洲语言库里找对应词并加以替换，使得这些思想得以在西方以外的国家传播开来。正如德勒兹所说：“‘替代’是赋予词语一种重要的超越本义的重复能力”。关于“替代”的探讨就到此为止，那么“伪装”这个主题呢？

“伪装”的主题是有关我们认知新事物、命名新事物的能力。在这个命题中，有好几组对立的事物都处在张力中：共性与重复、规律与诗、社会学与记忆。这些张力使我们认识到政治判断是如何寻求驯服新范畴的。

回过头再来看《庶民研究》的奠基文本——古哈的《殖民主义时期印度的农民起义的基本方面》一书。在古哈与霍布斯鲍姆关于农民和部族是否属于"'前政治时期'没有政治素养的公民"的论战中，"政治的"一词究竟如何归类？[23] 该状态很模棱两可：一方面，农民在与殖民统治政府斗争，我们说农民的斗争是"政治的"，我们是在用该词的固有含义；另一方面我们说农民的思维是"政治的"，我们是在用该词的引申义，于是就很难把握该词的真正含义了。我们说十九世纪农民起义是"政治的"，这种说法只有建立在我们全部人都已经完全知道"带有政治性"是什么意思的这种假设的基础上才能成立。我们只有通过"政治"这个旧的范畴的"伪装"才能表达出十九世纪印度的农民抵抗都有哪些新进展。

在十九世纪的澳大利亚也发生过一件极其相似的事。亨利·雷诺兹（Henry Reynolds）关于澳大利亚当地土著反抗白人统治的划时代著作让我们再次意识到问题并非欧洲人所想的那样是一种"处于'前政治时期'的没有政治素养的人"。在《自由人民的命运》一书中，雷诺兹以十九世纪澳大利亚塔斯马尼亚岛上的例子分析了当地土著部族对白人统治者的抗争。雷诺兹意识到了近代的政治观念的欧洲渊源。书中写道，很多白人殖民者在塔斯马尼亚统治期间惊异于当地部族"对自己自然权利的想法"，雷诺兹将此非常准确地看作欧洲人企图“以欧洲的方式”去诠释他们在土著人中遇到的造物过程。然而，在拒斥早期白人历史学家与编年史家所写的历史著作的同时，雷诺兹也像古哈一样坚持“政治的”这个范畴的适用性。雷诺兹公开挑战了“塔斯马尼亚人不具有参与政治行动能力”的观点，并特意描述了十九世纪当地土著部族的首领瓦尔特·阿瑟（Walter Arthur）。雷诺德称阿瑟是“第一个土著民族主义者”，并将民族主义的观念从其近代体制史的寄托中抽离出来。[24]显然“政治”与“民族主义”这两个范畴语焉不详、既有社会学的元素也有修辞的元素，不完全能够满足澄清的要求。正是在此种修辞的不精确中发生了对新事物的伪装。

兹于此再举我前面跟进过的帕沙·查特吉（Partha Chatterjee）对“被统治者”的范畴进行归类的例子。查特吉在演讲中用文献资料描述了当时印度加尔各答的“被统治者”在殖民时期每日为生存而抗争的情形（包括窃取电源），并突然在其演讲的末尾把印度殖民当局下的“被统治者”说成是缔造了甚至亚里士多德都可能会辨认出来的东西：民主。查特吉进一步写道：“我所要努力展示的是，除了群众主权的抽象承诺，世界上大部分的‘被统治者’还在发明新的方式，使自己可以选择被以何种方式统治”。他还承认，“政治社会的很多模式”以及在这些模式下的不合法的活动可能不会得到“亚里士多德的赞许”。但他认为，如果亚里士多德这个“睿智的希腊人”当年可以看到查特吉的证据，或许会在他会辨认出一些他所不赞成的大众行为背后所蕴藏的民主的伦理正当性。[25]我的观点还是：这一举动的模棱两可，以及主张当年加尔各答日常的群众行动看起来不总是民主的，但看起来依然预兆了未来的民主政体。当然，我们到现在还不能找出一个范畴去准确描述加尔各答的未来的日常生活。查特吉的文章中，正是在“民主”一词的新义和旧义那模棱两可的运用中，在加尔各答发生的“新事物”显现和隐蔽自身。我们时而看到时而看不到。

最后我为“伪装”这个主题再举一例。这就是著名的哈特与内格里（Hardt and Negri）所提出的“群众”（multitude）一词，该词亦是我认为可以替换描述欧洲革命主体的一个候选词。对于一本前半部分在苦苦地寻求描述世界上的主导——帝国——的书，伪装是具有反讽意味的。但是，作为革命主体的“群众”，尽管是以一种斯宾诺莎式的内在关联来构思的，可还是必须获得“充分的意识”（对黑格尔与马克思的回响）方能具有政治性。哈特和内格里问到：“如何让‘群众’的行为具有政治性？”他们的回答：“我们所能给出的唯一回应……就是要让‘群众’以‘充分的意识’直接应对帝国压迫性的核心运作的时候，他们就首要具备了政治性。”[26]

现在我必须提出最后的问题：为什么“替代”和“伪装”联合而创造出了“重复”的结构？我想这个问题马克思很早提到过。新事物是通过对判断与法律的挑战来到世界上的。这就是为什么德勒兹从诗的角度作为切入点来研究“重复”。政治判断往往都同旧事物存亡与共。记起霍米·巴巴是大有裨益的——甚至是这个对后殖民状况进行“生成调解”，对（传统上理解的）社会主义的斗争的条件没什么心得的理论家也是以一个后殖民理论家而起家的他企图与英国1980年代的社会主义政治相联系。[27] 我认为，马克思在反思历史中的重复与相似时——因而也反思了“滞后”，触及了新事物出现时所必须的伪装。这段话的确很出名，但可能对此处讨论的上下文中的重复有所关联，让我以马克思的话作结，加一个小小的限定性条件：

人类创造了自己的历史，然而并不是从心所欲的。死去的所有世代的传统像梦魇一样压在今人的头脑中。甚至正当他们着手创造一些未曾有的东西的时候，也要焦虑地乞灵于过去的神明，借用他们的名份、口号和行头，以便用这个确立已久的伪装和这一借来的语言呈现世界历史的新场景。

马克思希望这个过程有一个好的黑格尔式的结局。他把这一过程同一个人学习一门新语言的经历相比，他说：“一个学习外语的入门者总会把所学的外语翻译回母语。只有当他不需要借助对旧语言的回忆，并在使用新语言中忘却母语的时候，才能够吸收新语言的精神并用它自由表达自我。”[28] 我们有理由对这种好结局表示怀疑。我们依旧对总是回来纠缠翻译的成就的那些失败翻译的残余表示出兴趣。这就是我们在思考有关“重复”与“滞后”问题时要与马克思和他的徒子徒孙分道扬镳的地方。

感谢本书的编辑以及他们的建言。

(翻译：陈恒)

注释：

1 贝蒂·赛义德（Betty Seid），《新叙事：印度当代艺术》（*New Narratives: Contemporary Art from India*），Ahmedabad and Ocean Township，N.J.，Mapin 与 Grantha 出版，2007 年。

2 《新叙事》，第 13 页。

3 《新叙事》，第 15 页。

4 《新叙事》，第 19 页。

5 会议陈词，“（世界）艺术：艺术史与全球实践”，西北大学，2008 年 5 月 23-24 日。

6 亚历山大·格申克龙，《经济落后的历史透视—论文集》（*Economic Backwardness in Historical Perspective — A Book of Essays*），麻省剑桥，Bellknap Harvard 出版，1962 年。

7 霍米·巴巴，“新事物如何进入世界？”（How Does Newness Enter the World?），出自《文化的方位》（The Location of Culture）。

8 德勒兹，《差异与重复》，保罗·巴顿译，纽约，哥伦比亚大学出版社，1994 年，第 1 页。

9 德勒兹，《差异与重复》，1-2 页。

10 德勒兹《差异与重复》，第 10 页。

11 德勒兹《差异与重复》，第 xvi 页，第 7 页。

12 见 E·P·汤普森（E.P. Thompson），《辉格党和猎人》（*Whigs and Hunters*）。

13 我在“庶民研究简史”一文中有详述，见《近代化习惯——庶民研究的影响》（*Habitations of Modernity: Essays in the Wake of Subaltern Studies*）（芝加哥大学出版社，2002 年）一书第一章。

14 见我所著《地方化欧洲：后殖民思想与历史差异》（*Provincializing Europe: Postcolonial Thought and Historical Difference*）（普林斯顿大学出版社，2000 年）一书的引言部分。

15 详见《地方化欧洲》一书“导论”部分。

16 见贾南德拉·潘迪（Gyanendra Pandey）关于历史学家拉纳吉特·古哈的论文，以及加亚特里讷·斯皮瓦克（Gayatri Chakravorty Spivak）编，《庶民研究选编》（*Selected Subaltern Studies*），纽约，牛津大学出版社，1988 年。

17 弗兰切斯卡·奥西尼 (Francesca Orsini)，“20 世纪印度公共领域和政治话语”(The Hindi Public Sphere and Political Discourse in the Twentieth Century)，未发表论文，出席“南亚政治的方位”（The Sites of the Political in South Asia）会议时的讲话，柏林，2003 年 10 月。

18 同上。

19 对于这一点的上佳讨论，参见安德烈·瓦里克（Andrzej Walicki），《围绕资本主义的争论：有关俄罗斯民粹派的社会哲学研究》（*The Controversy Over Capitalism: Studies in the Social Philosophy of the Russian Populists*），印第安那，圣母大学出版社，1989 年，第一、二章，主要见“后退的好处”（The Privilege of Backwardness）一文。

20 拉纳吉特·古哈，《殖民时期印度农民起义的基本方面》（Elementary Aspects of Peasant Insurgency in Colonial India），德里，牛津大学出版社，1983 年，第 1 章。

21 沙希德·阿明（Shahid Amin），“对非西方历史的去隔离化”（*De-Ghettoising the Histories of the non-West*），吉安·普拉卡什（Gyan Prakash），“学术的方位”（The Location of Scholarship），我的“全球化、民主与历史的撤退？”(Globalization, Democracy, and the Evacuation of History?)，见杰奇·阿萨亚格 (Jackie Assayag) 和韦罗妮克·拜奈伊 (Veronique Benei) 编，《离散中的归来：南亚学者与西方》（*At Home in Diaspora: South Asian Scholars and the West*），布卢明顿，印第安纳大学出版社，2003 年。

22 弗朗茨·法农，《世界上悲惨的人》(*The Wretched of the Earth*)，康斯坦茨·法灵顿（Constance Farrington）译，纽约，格罗夫出版社，1963年，第40页。

23 拉纳吉特·古哈，《殖民时期印度的农民起义的基本方面》，第一章。

24 亨利·雷诺兹（Henry Reynolds），《自由民族的命运》（*Fate of a Free People*），灵伍德，维多利亚，企鹅出版社，1995年，第11页，23页，69页。

25 帕沙·查特吉，《被统治者的政治——世界大部分国家的主流政治之思》（*The Politics of the Governed: Reflections on Popular Politics in Most of the World*），纽约，哥伦比亚大学出版社，2004年，77-78页。

26 迈克尔·哈特（Michael Hardt）和安东尼·内格里（Antonio Negri），《帝国》（Empire），麻省剑桥，哈佛大学出版社，2000年，第399页。

27 霍米·巴巴，"对理论的奉献"(The Commitment to Theory)，出自《文化的方位》。

28 卡尔·马克思，"路易·波拿巴的雾月十八日"（The Eighteenth Brumaire of Louis Bonaparte），《马克思恩格斯选集》第一卷，莫斯科，进步出版社，1969年，第398页。

后殖民与历史的人造：
谁可以为“印度”的过去说话？

把思想推向极致。

——路易·阿尔都赛

一

人们最近在赞扬后殖民的《庶民研究》项目时，说它显示，“也许是自殖民化以来，人们首次看到，印度人正在展示重新运用（在历史学科中）表现自我的能力，并且这样的趋势还在延续”[1]。作为《庶民研究》小组的一员，我认为这一赞扬让人高兴，但现在得出这结论还为时过早。这篇文章的目的是将“印度人”“在历史中表现自我”这样一个观点问题化。首先让我们抛开像庶民研究这样一个转型课题所必要包含的许多认同问题，在这里，护照与承诺往往会以一种有些人会认为是后现代特有的方式模糊了民族的特征。但我要提出一个更悖逆的论点，即：就学术的历史话语——亦即作为在大学的体制场域中生产出来的话语的“历史”——而言，“欧洲”依然是在包括我们所谓“印度的”、“中国的”、“肯尼亚的”等等在内的所有历史中居于统领地位的理论主题。所有其它历史都会以一种很奇特的方式成为“欧洲的历史”这一主叙事（master narrative）的变体。从这个意义上来说，“印度的”历史本身就是处于庶民的地位，也唯有以这个历史的名义，我们才能够明晰地表达庶民主体的立场。

本文其余篇幅会对此命题加以深入阐述，这里我先加上几个限定。在此，“欧洲”和“印度”是作为超现实（hyperreal）的语汇处理的，因为它们指涉一种想象上的地方，其地理指涉对象依然是未确定的[2]。作为想象之物，它们当然可以有争辩的空间。不过，这里我是把它们当成是一种既定的、被规范的范畴，分别处在支配和从属的对立位置上。这样看待此一问题，我知道自己会被冠以自然主义、民族主义的名号，甚至是被认为是患上了万恶之首的乡愁病。自由派学者马上会表示抗议，他们认为，任何一种声称"欧洲"是同质的、无争议的说法经过他们的剖析都会被瓦解。确实有道理，但就跟东方主义的现象不会因为我们部分人开始对其产生批判的意识而消失一样，某一版本的"欧洲"，在日常的权力关系的现象世界中被具体化并作为现代的出生场域而得到颂扬，继续支配关于历史的话语。分析并不能消灭它。

欧洲被作为历史的一个无声的指涉对象这一事实本身也是在一种非常平淡的状态下发生的。在非西方的第三世界国家历史学庶民研究里，至少有两样症状每天都在发生，即第三世界国家的历史学家感觉到需要以欧洲的历史作为参照，但欧洲的历史学家则从来没有感到要拿第三国家的历史作为参照。不管是爱德华·汤姆逊（Edward Thompson）、埃马纽埃尔·勒华拉杜里（Le Roy Ladurie），乔治·杜比（George Duby），卡洛·金斯伯格（Carlo Ginzberg），劳伦斯·斯通（Lawrence Stone），罗伯特·达恩顿（Robert Darnton），或娜塔莉·戴维斯（Natalie Davis）——就随便举几个名字——那些成功的历史学研究必然是对欧洲的研究。"他们"

的工作基本上昧于非西方的历史，这看起来并未影响到他们的研究质量本身。这样一种姿态，“我们”无法以其人之道还治于其人之身了。我们甚至要冒“老套”或“过时”的恶名，才可在这个层面上表现出一种等价的、相对应的无知。

而这样的问题，我想插一句，不仅仅限于历史学家。另外一个非自觉的但同样露骨的例子发生在文学研究领域，以下是近来一本论述后现代主义的文本中有关萨尔曼·拉什迪的一句话：“虽然《午夜之子》里的萨尔曼·拉什迪是用英语讲述他的故事，但是他的历史书写跟文学书写的互文性却是加倍的：一方面是来源于历史的传奇、电影和文学，另一方面是来源于西方，包括《铁皮鼓》、《项迪传》和《百年孤独》，如此等等。”[3]有趣的是，这个句子仅仅是梳理了来自“西方”的征引。作者在此并无任何的义务去指明到底是怎样的“印度”征引使得拉什迪的互文性呈现出“加倍”。这样一种共通且默认的漠视，正是使得拉什迪的作品很“容易”成为开设后殖民课程的英语系的默认契约的一部分。

不对称的漠视的问题不仅仅是我们自身“文化懦弱”（用我澳大利亚自我的话来说）的表现，也不是欧洲历史学家的文化傲视姿态。这些问题确实是存在的，但是可以比较容易的处理。我也不是希望要把那些刚才提到过的历史学家的功绩给抹去。我们的脚注充分证明了他们的知识与创造力给我们带来的启发。而“欧洲”成为所有历史学的主导主题本身则是另外一个更为深刻的理论条件，即第三世界中的史学知识生产的条件的一部分。这一条件通常有一种吊诡的自我表达方式。这一吊诡我将其描述为我们的庶民性（subalternity）的第二个日常表征，它指向社会科学的表述的本质。

过去的若干世代里，哲学家和思想家关于社会科学的思辨所产生的理论涵盖了人文科学的全部。但是我们知道，这些陈述是在忽略大多数人的存在之基础上得出的，有时是被相对的忽略，有时是被完全忽略。这本身并不吊诡。因为那些更自觉的欧洲哲学家总是会从理论上来为这样一种立场辩护。但第三世界社会科学的吊诡在于，我们发现，这些理论对于理解我们的社会是极为有用的，虽然理论本身是忽略了“我们”的存在的。那又是什么使得欧洲的圣哲，在实证阙如的情况下，也能发展出那样超凡的洞察力？为什么我们就不能回以凝视（return the gaze）？

我们可以在一些哲人关于历史的著述中找到答案。他们从欧洲历史中解读出了一种普世理性的实体形式（entelechy）——假如我们把哲学论述看成是社会科学的自我意识的话。他们的观点是，只有“欧洲”是从理论上可知的（比如，在最基础的层面所塑造的历史思维，其他国家的历史实证研究所得出的理论框架最终都是“欧洲”的框架。埃德蒙德·胡塞尔（Edmund Husserl）于1935年在维也纳做的一个演讲就包含了这样的论调，他说，“东方哲学”（更具体的是指印度和中国的哲学家）与“希腊——欧洲科学”（或者像他所说的，“广义上的哲学”）之间最根本的差异在于，后者有能力创造出“绝对的理论洞见”，也就是“**theoria**”（普遍适用的科学），而前者则只是“实践—普世”，因而会更具“神秘和宗教”色彩。这样一种“实践——普世”的哲学所对应的是一种“幼稚”和“直观”的世界观。有了“**theoria**”，这个世界就是“可主题化”的，使得“通过普遍适用的科学理性以提升人类”[4]的实践（praxis）成为可能。

同样的认识论基础也见于马克思关于“资产阶级”、“前资产阶级”或“资本”、“前资本”等范畴概念的使用。这里的前缀“前”代表的关系同时是时间上和理论上的。马克思在《政治经济学批判大纲》和其他地方所提到的资产阶级或资本主义社会的到来，使得人们第一次可以通过哲学和“资本”这一普遍范畴来理解历史。也就是说，历史第一次变得从理论上可理解了。过去所有的历史（从理论上讲）都可以通过这样一个范畴来理解，也就是说，可以从他们各自在“资本”上的差异来理解。而事物只会在发展到最成熟的时候显示出其范畴属性，或者像马克思在《政治经济学批判大纲》里所写的：“人的解剖包含了猿人解剖的钥匙”[5]。我在别的地方有论述过，“资本”这一范畴，其本身就包含了文艺复兴的思想印迹[6]。也不奇怪，马克思在《资本论》第一卷第一章里所写的那段很黑格尔式的文字，就说道，“资本”的秘密，“直到人类平等获得一种普遍偏见的固定性之后，才能获得破解。”[7]马克思继续写到：

即使是最为抽象的范畴，尽管它们是合理的，但正是因为它们的抽象，因而对于所有的世代来说，都是一种历史关系的产物。资产阶级社会是发展最为成熟最为复杂的生产组织形态。其范畴反映出其关系，其结构之全面，使得我们也可以窥视到历史上曾经有过但业已消亡的社会结构和生产形态，因为资产阶级也是在这些结构和形态基础上建立起来的，并且那些旧的结构中尚未完全被征服的一部分依然留存至今，那些本来只是琐碎的细节今日则发展成为了资产阶级社会中的重要成分。如此等等。只有等到更高一级的社会发展之后，低级动物族群如何通过模仿而发展的过程才能被理解。因此，资产阶级社会的经济提供了我们理解古代的重要钥匙[8]。

对于“资本”或是“资产阶级”，我建议，读作“欧洲”。

二

不管是马克思还是胡塞尔，都没有本着一种历史主义的精神在说话——至少在上述的引文里没有体现。在引文里，我们可以看到，马克思的愿景是通过摆脱资本的统治来达到解放，甚至是超越法律上的平等，虽然后者被自由主义看作是神圣不可侵犯。“各尽其能，各尽所需”这句格言与“同工同酬”是恰恰相反的，这也是为什么马克思会同时批评资本主义和自由主义——不管是在有柏林墙和柏林墙不复存在的年代——因而马克思的思想都会渗透到任何关于后殖民、后现代的历史创作中。但是马克思的方法论和认识论论述不能够拒斥历史的解读。这样的理论总是有大量模糊不清的地方，使得“马克思主义”的历史叙事得以浮现。这些叙事都是围绕“历史转折”展开的。大多数的现代第三国家的历史叙事都离不开这样的历史转折所带来的诸多问题。其中最突出的话题是发展、现代化以及资本主义（虽然这些话题经常是隐含在话语之下）。

这样的一种倾向在我们的”庶民研究”项目里也有所体现。我写的关于工人阶级的历史的书就遇到了同样的问题[9]。苏米特·萨卡尔(Sumit Sarkar)(他是”庶民研究”的另外一位同人)所写的《现代印度》一书被公认为讲述印度历史的最好的大学教科书之一，该书开头写到:

从1885年印度国大党诞生到1947年8月印度取得独立，这六十多年见证了我们这一国家在漫长历史上也许最为重要的一个转折。这一转折，从很多方面看，还未曾完成，是不是正因为这样一个中心性的模糊使得我们可以最为方便的开展我们的调查？[10]

那是怎样的一种转折到今天依然没有完成？萨卡尔暗示可能会有很几个，他在书里列出了如下三个:

在争取国家独立进程当中所提出的很多理想现今依然没有兑现，比如甘地那个让农民作主人的设想，还有是社会革命所留下的许多理想。而印度、巴基斯坦（以及孟加拉国）的历史一再表明，资产阶级获得翻身，资本主义获得成功的发展这样的问题都不是因为1947年权力移交而马上得到解决的。

不管是农民阶级那个神秘正义王国的梦想，或者是左派的社会（主义）革命理想，或者是“全面资产阶级转型”都没有得到兑现。萨卡尔所描述的“未完成”正是在此三者的缺位之下而存在的。

也是由于类似的对“缺位”的指涉，历史终于没有能如人们设想那样奉天承运（这是否又是“懒惰的本地人”之体现？）。在这样的背景下，我们提出了”庶民研究”的课题：

这是关于**一个国家不能兑现自身的承诺**、它是因为资产阶级阶级以及工人阶级没有**足够**的力量将国家带向对抗殖民主义的决定性的胜利，以及关于19世纪经典的——或现代的——资产阶级民主革命的研究。而正是**对于这一失败的研究成为了殖民时期印度历史地图的核心问题**[11]。

在上述的选段里，作者以缺乏、不在场、不完整的眼光来看待印度历史，结果得到的是一种“不完整”。这样一种叙事的方式其实可以上溯到印度殖民统治的早期。英国征服了印度，并且忽视印度之多元性，而以一种一元化的讲述，称那是从“中世纪”到“现代”的转型。这样的术语也随着时间的发展而不断衍生出新的讲法。人们曾把“中世纪”称作“残酷的暴君”，把“现代”理解为“法治”。而“封建 / 资本主义”这样的区分则是后来衍生出来的。

而当这样的观点在殖民统治下的印度确立之后，关于转折的叙说其实是对帝国主义者的暴力和征服的毫不掩饰的颂扬。这里仅举一个例子，亚历山大 · 道尔所写的《印度斯坦历史》，其前三卷最先于 1770 至 1772 年间出版，就是为国王而写的。那时候也不需要像福柯这样的人来揭示暴力与知识之间的联系。道尔如此写到：“国王陛下军队之成就，为那些好奇的研究者打开了东方的大门。”[12] 为了强调暴力和现代性之联系，道尔还写道：

英国已经成为了孟加拉的征服者，他们应当对该国的部分基本法律加以修改，使得他们的政府拥有合法的基础。一朝拥有宝剑，我们就是统治者。这是绝对的征服，全世界也同样认为。

道尔在他的书里将这样一种“基本法律”就是与过去的那种“任意的”“暴政”统治形成反差的“法治”。道尔在详细的叙述了解释说，“暴政”并不是指“只会随意行使权力的政府”，因为他对印度历史很熟悉，知道那不是印度历史之真相。“暴政”是英国立宪政府的反面，“暴政”是一种“立法、司法和行政三种权力同时归国王掌管”的机制。过去就是这样一种缺乏自由的状态。而随着英国殖民统治的开始，印度被转变成为一个法律体，管理这一国家的政府将会受到私人财产（此乃“公共繁荣之根基”，道尔如此说道）以及公共舆论的压力，同时也受到一个法制机构的约束，这一机构“行使法律维护正义，它必须独立于法律以外的任何东西，否则（法官）就会变为暴政政权压迫人民的工具。”

在19到20世纪，属于精英阶层的印度民族主义者发现，他们的民族主义者身份在这一转型期的叙事中，在不同的时期和因应自身意识形态之不同，在暴政与宪政、中世纪与现代、封建与资本主义的中间，往往就隔着“印度历史”。在这样一种帝国主义者与民族主义者共同认可的叙事里，“印度”通常是以缺失的形象出现的。换而言之，在此类的叙述中，总是有一些代表土著的声音，这些声音说反映的就是“不足”或“失败”这样的主题。道氏在为孟加拉 / 印度 提出的“法治”的同时，对英国方面却提出了矛盾的承诺，称并没有在印度本土居民中间“融入自由的精神”：

要让孟加拉这片沃土上的人们取得自由，这超出了政治架构的力所能及范围。这里的宗教、这里的社会机构、社会道德风俗以及民众的心智，使得孟加拉的人民养成了一种臣民的心态。给他们财产权只会使得他们和我们的利益绑定得更加深厚，使得他们成为我们的臣仆，或者用英国人更喜欢的说法，成为我们的奴隶。

我们可以确证，（印度人）在未来多年内所享有的是臣民的权利，而非公民的权利，这将成为大英帝国意识形态的基石。印度人从来就不享有公民的权利，他们不配享有。这样的理论也会成为自由派理论的一部分[13]。这也正是民族主义者与我们的分歧所在。不管是罗姆莫罕·罗易（Rammohun Roy）还是班基姆钱德拉·查托帕迪亚雅（Bankimchandra Chattopadhyay），对于这两位19世纪印度最著名的民族主义知识分子来说，大英帝国的殖民是印度必须经历的一个时期，唯有经过这样一个修炼的过程，印度人才会获得公民以及国家的身份认同——虽然英国一直在鼓吹这一身份认同，但直到最后依然没有给到印度。很久以后的1951年，一位成功地出卖他的"无名"的"不为人知"的印度人这样向他的一生致辞：

是英属印度帝国

将臣民身份赋予了我们

却剥夺了我们的公民权

我们要纪念它

为了这个

我们每个人都得接受这个挑战

"与大英国民同等"

因为

我们所拥有的珍贵的东西

都是

经由同样的英国统治

塑造、锤炼和打造出来的[14]。

帕沙·查特吉的研究显示，在民族主义者的叙事里，只有农民和工人以及庶民阶层，才需要承担“不足”的十字架。这样一种理论认为，只有这些人才是需要接受教育，通过教育来消除他们的无知、狭隘或虚伪的思想形态的[15]。即使是在今天，这个由英语、印地语混合而成的“社群主义”这个词指的是那些没能够得上“世俗”的公民理念的人。

英国的统治给印度的土地带来了资产阶级个人主义的实践、机构以及话语，这些都是不可否认的。在1830年代以及1840年代的早期——当民族主义尚未兴起的时候，对渴望成为“法律主体”的表述是——要成为一个“现代人”就是要成为一个“欧洲人”。《文学拾遗》（The Literary Gleaner）是殖民时期加尔各答的一本杂志，它曾于1842年刊载了以下这首诗，诗歌是用英语写的，作者是孟加拉的一位学生，他写这首诗的时候18岁。可以看出，这首诗显然是因为受到轮船离开孟加拉，驶向“英格兰的光荣海岸”的景象之刺激而写的。

我常常像悲伤的小鸟那样歌唱

离开这片土地，虽然它是我的故土

绿油油的草地，鲜亮的花朵、万里无云的晴空
虽然安逸，于我却无半丝吸引
因为我梦想着更为明亮和自由的钟声
那里充满了美德，自由
使得即使最底层的人也感到幸福

看不到有人为了讨饭掰断双膝
科学昌明，贤者受器重
人人皆得活出最美好真实的自我
大自然无比甜美
但我只能空想
我情愿在那样的国度生和死[16]

这首诗能够让人窥见弥尔顿以及十七世纪英国激进主义的影子，它显然是一首殖民的杂凑之作[17]。诗的作者是迈克尔·马杜苏登·杜特（Michael Madhusudan Dutt），这位年轻的孟加拉诗人后来终于意识到成为“欧洲人”的不可能，于是回归到孟加拉文学当中，并且成为了他那个时代最优秀的诗人之一。其后的印度人则开始抛弃这样一种对成为“欧洲人”的疯狂的追求。民族主义恰恰就是在基于让所有人都能成为个人的基础上诞生的，它的预设就是，“个人权利”以及抽象的“平等”都是普世的价值，都能在世界上任何一个地方找到，一个人可以同时是“印度人”

以及一个“公民”。我们接下来还会分析这一项目本身的自身矛盾之处。

现代个人主义的很多公共和私人典仪在十九世纪即已变得可见。有人将四种自我表达的方式的出现看作是这一潮流兴起的标志。这四种表达方式是：小说、传记、自传以及历史[18]。伴随这些同时出现的还有现代工业、技术、医学、类资产阶级的法律体系（本质上是殖民色彩的）——由国家给予支持，其后被民族主义接管，并创造出有其特色的新的体系。我一直在讲述的转型期的故事，则成为这些机构的根基，反过来也受到这些机构的制约。我们可以将这些机构看作是一个金字塔，在最顶端的是现代国家，[19] 而一旦提到现代国家，我们则必然会想到一个理论主体为欧洲的历史。甘地在 1909 年的时候就明白了这一点。在甘地所写的《印度自治》一书里，当他提到民族主义要求更多的铁路、现代药物、以及资产阶级，他非常犀利的指出，这些做法都是要“使印度变得英国化”，或者用他的原话，就是“没有英国人的英国式治理”[20]。这样的一个“欧洲”，当然只是由殖民者向被殖民者传递的一种故事，在迈克尔·马杜苏登·杜特的那首诗里显现得非常明显，这么做也完全是为了殖民统治的需要[21]。甘地对“欧洲”的批评，也因为他的民族主义背景而不甚彻底，同时我也没有特别钟爱他的文章的倾向。但是我觉得他的这样一种姿势是有用的，特别是对于研究非都市史而言是很有意义的。

三

现在我要回到“失败”、“缺乏”、“不足”这些一旦谈及“印度”历史就会出现的主题上。正如起义的农民要反抗殖民统治的印度一样，事情起步必须是由一个叛逆的姿势开始的[22]。让我们从转型叙述结束的地方开始，重新去解读出“丰富”与“创造力”，而非我们一直所解读的“缺乏”与“不足”。

根据宪法，印度人如今是“公民”。这样一个宪法是使用了经典的对公民权的最自由的定义。假如现代国家和现代人，现代公民，是不可分割的同一现象的两面——就像威廉·康诺利在《政治理论与现代性》里所分析的那样——那么我们似乎可以看到历史在印度的终结了[23]。现代人的政治 / 公共生活是一种公民生活，他比然也会有一个内在的“私人”生活，这些可以在他的自己、书信、自传、小说以及我们对被观察者的谈话中得以记录。资产阶级式的个人只有在人们发现了私人生活之快乐之后才会成为可能。但这又是非常特殊的一种“私人”——它实际上是一种退化的“公共”，哈贝马斯就曾提醒过我们，这样一种资产阶级的生活，“总是在面对着一个观众（**大众**）（Publikum）”[24]。

印度的公共生活也许是对法律虚构出来的公民生活的模仿——这样的虚构在现实的印度通常是以一种喜剧的形式实现的——但资产阶级私人生活和它的历史又该怎么理解呢？任何人只要写过“法国”社会历史，并且其中包含了印度相关的材料，就会明白那是多么困难的一件事情[25]。不是说资产阶级的私人生活没有欧式的法则。自从19世纪中叶以来，就有了印度小说、日记、书信、自传等。但是他们很少会描写真正的私人生活。男人写的自传都非常的“公共化”（其中对公共生活的描写也不见得很现代），而女人写的自传则会讲述直系家族的故事[26]。总之，那种忏悔式的自传非常鲜见。尼拉德·乔杜里（Nirad Chaudhuri）写了一部被受推崇也曾获奖的自传，但是对于他的新婚之夜的描写只有一段（全书有963页），我们可以拿这个作为例子，并且可以大段的引用。首先得介绍一下，这是一个由父母安排的婚姻(孟加拉，1932年），乔杜里当时感到非常的紧张，因为他害怕自己的妻子不能欣赏自己刚刚才开始的西方古典音乐收藏癖。因为他的文章的内在联系的逻辑我们无法搞清楚，所以我们也难以理解乔杜里——也许有一种宗教上的对“过分”暴露的回避在其中发挥着作用。但是这段文字还是很好的一段回忆，因为它是乔杜里对于他的第一夜的回忆。他会用“我不记得”“我不知道怎么样”这些字眼来回避一些私密片段的描写（更不用提弗洛伊德式的和盘托出了),这样一个自我构建的面纱显然也是作者个性的一部分:

要见一个陌生的女子，并且她要成为我的妻子，我想到这就很不自在。当她被带进房间，并且走到我身边站着的时候，我一句话也没有说。我只看到她脸上很羞涩的笑容，她小心翼翼的走过来，和我坐在床的边上。我不知道我们后来是怎么溜到枕头旁，并且肩并肩躺下来的。（乔杜里在脚注里写到：“当然，我们都穿着衣服。我们都是印度教徒，我们相信，严整的衣冠和完全的暴露都是很合适的，但在此二者之间的任何一个状态都是不合适的。没有一个认真的男人会挑逗他的妻子。”）我们接着开始讲话。她拿起我的手臂，摸了摸，说：“你真瘦。我要好好的照顾你。”我没有感谢她，甚至除了听到这几个字以外，我还有被抚摸的感觉。这时，我脑子里响起了欧洲音乐……[27]

在乔杜里的两卷自传里，对“现代”的渴望跳跃在字里行间。他的名字现在是印度—英国文化交往历史的象征。但是在这样一本1500多页的自传里，这是唯一一段写到乔杜里的私人生活的文字，前后都是关于他公共生活的描写。我们该如何去解读这段文字，它是一位执着于展现自己的公共生活的印度男子的写照，但是却很少，甚至没有在写作上展现过现代公民的另一种生活，即私人生活不由自主的外在表露。能够有纯粹的公共生活而没有私人生活吗？这是不是印度资产阶级转变的另外一种“不足”？

这些问题都是由转型期的叙述所带出来的，它同时也把现代的个体放到了历史的末端。我不希望从乔杜里的自传里读出一些他本来没有的含义。我之前已经指出过，女性的写作是不一样的。学者也才刚刚开始研究反映出印度历史的一些自传。而假如欧洲在印度的殖民化统治的其中一个结果是引进现代国家制度以及归属于国家的“子民”，而“子民的权利”（例如“法治”），就把现代的个体分割为“公共”与“私人”两部分（马克思年轻的时候所写的《论犹太问题》一文里就曾提到），这些主题跟其他的一些关于自我以及社群的叙述是联系在一起的，虽然彼此之间会有斗争、联合和分裂[28]。这本身是不具争议性的，但我的想法是更进一步的。也就是，其他这些关于个人以及社群的叙述虽然也有记录的价值，但他们不能提供一些关于历史的基础的叙述。这部分是因为这些叙述通常是暗含了反历史的倾向。他们的叙事主体以及回忆都让人不得不反问这是否属于历史。而“历史”则正是以现代的名义吞噬了这一类记忆的家伙。

接下来我要通过对一段颇具争议性的历史的叙述，来论证这一观点，这一故事体现的正是现代私人生活与公共生活在殖民时期的印度之紧密相连[29]。

四

接下来要展示的是孟加拉在殖民时期的资产阶级化过程的一个剪影。主要的文本写于1850年至1920年期间，主要是教授维多利亚时期的“家庭内务”——阅读这些文本的是印度孟加拉的中产阶层，是当时的一些显赫家族的人。大英帝国的统治将国家、市民社会、资产阶级家庭等现代政治结构渗透到民众生活当中。因此我们看到诸如资产阶级的家政、隐私以及个人主义都是通过大英帝国的统治带进印度的。这里我只是想提出印度人对这些外来理念的一些反抗和修改，他们 所反抗的也就是隐含在“现代性”

底下的两个基本的支柱，其一为基于婚恋的核心家庭，其二为世俗的、对时间的历史构建。

正如梅瑞迪斯·波兹维克，古兰·莫拾得以及其他的学者所指出的那样，18世纪的欧洲对“文明”的解释其后成为了在19世纪初以帝国俯视的方式批判印度家庭生活的武器，因为最值得追求的是维多利亚中期那种资产阶级式的家庭生活[30]。“妇女的状况”以及关于“现代”个人、“自由”、“平等”、“权利”等思想成为批判的武器。在詹姆斯·密尔（约翰·斯图亚特·密尔之父）所写的《英属印度历史》（1817年）一书里，家庭/国家以及更遥远的“自由”被作者绑在一起了：

妇女的生活状况是衡量一个国家是否文明的重要的因素……在那些未开化的社会里，妇女基本都是被驱使去做奴隶，随着文明的到来她们的妇女身份才慢慢得以显现。这一相对更弱的性别的生存状况逐步得到改善，直到他们可以获得和男人同等的待遇，并且可以自愿的去从事她们能力可以胜任的工作。而要找到一个比印度妇女那种被严厉限制和侮辱的更为糟糕的生存状况则基本是不可设想的[31]。

众所周知，印度的中产阶级觉得他们需要对这一指控负责。于是从19世纪中叶开始，他们在孟加拉（以及其他的一些地区）推行改革，改善妇女的生存状况，并且为妇女提供正式的教育。

很多人谈到这场妇女教育运动的时候所使用的词语都是称它具有革命性意义，并且使用了“自由”、“平等”、“觉醒”等词语，整一场运动也很大程度上受到了拉斯金式的理想与对资产阶级家庭生活的理想化[32]。假如我们将此看成是现代印度的个人奋斗史一部分，就会发现有很有趣的模式浮现出来。正是在一些关于这场妇女教育运动的文献中，我们看到了人们对一些词语进行了很热烈的辩论。将家庭生活的规律性以及卫生状况作为现代性的表现，这一点基本没有非议。但是，另外一个非常重要的词，自由，却没有很容易得到广泛的认同。对于这个词，很多人有不同的理解，并且这决不单单是两性之间的简单争斗。这个词被民族主义者们用来区分“欧洲人”与“印度人”。这一辩论对于发展出一套话语策略，使得主体可以以“印度人”的身份来说话非常重要。而接下来我正是想谈论一下这一主体性。

孟加拉文学对于女性教育的描述，一方面是民族主义关于父系、父权文化的构建，另一方面是资产阶级式核心家庭的描述，这正是欧洲 / 殖民者 / 普世价值倡导者在论及个人主义、公民权以及公民社会的时候使用得最多的词汇[33]。“纪律”与“秩序”对于民族主义者来说是美感与力量的重要组成部分。纪律被认为是殖民（也就是现代）政府权力的核心，但这需要一些步骤来完善。大英帝国很强大，因为它的国民非常有纪律，讲秩序并且守时。而正是通过对妇女的教育，才使得这样的美德被带到家庭。而传统印度的家庭，在民族主义者的笔下，则显得非常狼狈。我们看看下面这段写于 1877 年介绍妇女教育的孟加拉文字：

任何一个文明的欧洲人的家都像是诸神的居所。家里所有的东西都是洁净的，摆放整齐，装点优美；没有半点不洁或恶臭。仿佛是秩序之神 srinkhala 显形并且要取悦于人。在房子中央会有一张桌子，上面铺着一块桌布，桌布上摆放着鲜花，桌子边上是几张擦拭得非常洁净的椅子。而来到印度你会觉得自己仿佛是被指派去赎罪。首先闻到的是牛粪的臭味，空气中布满了尘土，屋子的角落里堆积起灰烬，还有四处在飞的苍蝇。你还能看到男孩在地上撒尿，而后再将自己的手放到上面。置身其间，仿佛进入了一个臭气横飞的地方，没有任何的秩序，看到屋子里的物品，没有一件是干净的，让人不觉作呕。”[34]

这样一种殖民叙述包含了两方面，一方面它看得出目前是混乱的状态，另一方面要走出这一状态只能走到一个想象中的“历史”未来。它实际上是一个预演，背景是殖民时期的资产阶级家庭生活，跟我们之前遇到的转型叙述是一样的。一个历史观的对某一短暂历程（如从中世纪向现代的转折）的记述，这也是殖民主体出现分化的地方。换而言之，历史就是不断的分裂，而写历史就是不断的去演绎这样的分裂。

这样一种对居家秩序的追求也因此可以看作是民族主义与现

代化渴望在公共场合下交织的产物，并且这是被国家权力强制执行的。当然探讨那样的话题已经超出了本文的范围。但是，个人纪律以及公共生活中的纪律之间的关系可以从民族主义者关于家庭卫生以及公共卫生的文字里看出脉络。其关联是如此的具有现代性，也是现代的印度人与现代欧洲人共有的一个特点[35]。但我希望说说他们之间的不同。于是我就得回到欧洲现代性的另一个重要方面，即关于“自由”与“平等”的叙述。

关于“自由”的辩论，围绕的是维多利亚时期关于美好婚姻的讨论，也就是说，妻子是不是也应当成为丈夫的朋友。因为没有其他的观点比这一个更能威胁孟加拉 / 印度宗族家庭（或者说是在这样的家庭里的岳母），这个观点往往是包含在资产阶级式的隐私关系里的，也就是说，妻子可以成为丈夫的朋友，也就是说，妻子也可以成为独立的个体。另外需要指出的是，现代的个体，当他 / 她声称自己拥有独立性的时候，总是出现在 19 世纪和 20 世纪初的孟加拉文学上，并且总是以矛盾的角色出现，成为被嘲笑的对象，虽然同样一篇小说也许颂扬的就是在公共以及私人生活中的纪律以及科学理性。这样的一种讽刺有多种表达方式。最出名反映出这一现代个体矛盾特点的小说角色就是尼姆钱德·达塔（Nimchand Datta），她是迪南般度·米特拉（Dinabandhu Mitra）所写的《Sadhabar ekadashi》（1866 年）里的角色。达塔接受过英国教育，一有机会就会引用莎士比亚、米尔顿、洛克的名句，并且因为这样的教育背景而对自己的家族管制置之不理。另外，达塔还喜欢喝酒和嫖妓。一方面是对“现代”/英式教育的热爱，另一方面是对酒精的沉迷，二者的关系可以从剧中达塔与孟加拉一位警官的对话可以看出来。Nimchand 开始是夸夸其谈的说自己英语怎么棒，但很快他就讲到了喝酒（要知道，在中产孟加拉文化里，喝酒就等同于堕落）：

我用英语读、用英语写、用英语说、用英语想、用英语做梦——要知道，这可不是小儿科。好吧，现在请告诉我，我的伙伴们，你们想喝什么？女的要干红葡萄酒，男的要雪利酒，而英雄们就给他们白兰地吧[36]。

我们在谈及妇女教育的文献中也看到了类似的关联，即现代的、“自由”的个人与自私的个人的对比。很明显的是，这样 的一种构建是民族主义色彩的（也是父系主义的）。人们以前曾用是否拥有自由来区分印度人与欧洲人/英国人。一个极度自由的印度女人的行为就跟一个 **memsahib**（欧洲女人）相似，都是自私而且厚颜无耻。正如 康达马拉·戴维（Kundamala Devi），一个专门为女性杂志《Bamabodhini patrika》撰稿的女人在 1870 年的时候所说，“假如您曾获得过知识，请不要**像 memsahib 那样**做女人，这可不是孟加拉女人的做法。”[37] 而“绝对谦逊”被用来建立这样的孟加拉女人的形象[38]。英迪拉·戴维（Indira Devi）在 1920 年的时候写了一篇叫“**女性发声**”的文章，并且将这篇文章献给 了她心目中的理想化的孟加拉女人：“不被天生所局限，谈吐得体，乐于奉献，不追逐个人享乐，却很容易被他人的痛苦所感动，即使拥有很少，却很快活。”[39]

这个描述里的“现代”孟加拉 / 印度女人，受过良好的教育，可以理解现代文明对身体和国家的约束，但是，她们又十分的“谦卑”，既不过于自信也不自私，而后者正是和关于“自由”的辩论联系在一起的。很多人认为，“自由”在西方的语文里就是 jathechhachar 的意思，可以根据自己的意愿做事情，以及可以沉溺自我。而在印度传统里，自由的意思是去除自我，自愿的去服侍他人和遵守命令。大家请注意看看下面的段落中，自由和奴役是如何转换了位置的：

人类自由的第一要务，乃在于屈尊，要屈从他人或**道德规范**（dharma），以及将心灵从感官的刺激中解放出来。正因为如此，在印度的家庭里，男孩和女孩都是要屈从父母的，妻子是要屈从丈夫和公公的，徒弟是要屈从师傅的，学生是要屈从老师的，国王则需屈从**道德规范**，臣民则需屈从国王，个人的尊严则需屈从于社区（samaj）[40]。

这里有一个比较讽刺性的转折是需要知道的。因为非常显然，“服侍他者的自由”对家里的仆人并不管用，在同样的一篇文章里，这些仆人还被认为是“真正”的非自由。这也是很多欧洲的观察家 所忽视的一点，他们并没有看到家里的妇女跟 家里的仆人二者之间的区别。很显然，在民族主义者的想象里，他们那时还未曾把仆人纳入考虑的范围。

就是在这样的背景之下，孟加拉作家去描写印度的家庭琐碎，正值印度的民间社会和类现代国家开始将诸如“公共”与“私人”这样的现代问题植入到 孟加拉中产的生活里面。传统的资产阶级式的关于家庭以及家国关系的看法在这里受到了两方面的重要冲击：策略之一是将传统的父系家族观念延伸到资产阶级关于父系家庭的概念当中，通过对旧体系的重新解释来取代新的价值观念。同样是按照这套思路来走的还包括现代个体。另外一个策略同等重要，它就是要调动一些集体记忆，去挑战“神圣”与“世俗”之间的绝对隔离，后者也恰恰是现代欧洲历史的基石[41]。那些“真正受到过教育”“真正谦逊”“真正具有印度特点”的女人获得器重，她们可以将家庭问题化为宗教问题，亦即把宗教上神圣的女性与那些肮脏的进行对比，而这样的对比只能是反历史的。

真正的现代家庭主妇，她象征的是像吉祥天女（Lakshmi）那样的神圣形象，整个家庭［族群，延伸这下还包括国家，**天女之子民**（Bharatlakshmi）］都是在她的光辉之下得到滋润和发展。于是我们可以在现代的一些传单上读到这样的文字：“女人就是国家的吉祥天女，假如她们可以在**道德**与知识上有所提升，那么整个社会的生活质量都会得到提升。”[42]吉祥天女在公元400年左右被认为是印度教大神毗湿奴的妻子，曾长期在印度教倍受重视，在普通的印度教家庭，更是被当成家庭妇女的道德榜样。她会在自愿的前提下，忠于其丈夫（以及他的家庭）[43]。假如女人不遵守这样的守则，那么整个家族都会被吉祥天女的神灵所灭，吉祥天女所象征的正是完全相反的道德准则。虽然女性的教育以及纪律在殖民时期的孟加拉很少会被反对，但是这一条界限却是在现代性以及资产阶级式隐私对家族传统带来动摇和冲击的时候划定的。

这里叙事的主体是民族主义以及父权主义的，用东方学的话语来说，就是“东方”与“西方”[44]。但是，我们最关心的是这一主体性所反映出来的两种否定：对资产阶级私人生活的否定以及对历史时间的否定。因为她们把家庭变成了一个神圣与世俗可以相融合的场所，但其遵循的规律还是神圣的诫条。

而反历史所带出的文化空间也并非和谐或无冲突的，虽然民族主义者会尝试这样去描述。父系家庭的反历史模式，唯有经过妇女本身以及庶民阶层的斗争，才能获得一席之地。但是这样的斗争不一定是你死我活的斗争。因为现代印度个体遭遇了太多的困境，不会如此直接的走到那一步。

这里我没有太多时间来展开这一话题，仅仅是给大家举一个例。这个例子来自 拉巴芭 · 拉纳德（Ramabai Ranade）的自传，她是19世纪著名的社会改革家拉纳德（M.G. Ranade）的妻子。拉巴芭·拉纳德所追求的其实就是脱离传统的父系家庭，而走进现代的新式婚姻，这也是她那改革派的丈夫所最喜欢看到的婚姻模式。为了追求这一目标，拉巴芭也会参与一些公共生活，并且会参加一些聚会，为男女社会改革者们提供咨询。正如她自己说的：“正是参加了这些聚会，才使得我懂得什么叫聚会，并且懂得如何在聚会上恪守礼仪。”[45] 有趣的是，那些反对拉巴芭如此做法的阻力当中最重要的一股力量（除了男人）是来自于她的家庭里的其他女人。很显然，家庭里的其他女人（她的岳母、她丈夫的姐妹）还是在为旧的父系家庭说话。但是听听这些姐妹的声音也是有意义的，因为她们也在说出自己的抗争：

你不该去参加这样的聚会……哪怕是男人让你去做什么事，你甭管就是了。也不需说不。不去作就是。他们最后就会放弃的，因为他们也会觉得无聊……你现在做得比欧洲的女人还要过分了。

还有这一段：

“是不是她真的喜欢这样的聚会呢？拉纳德先生也不是那么热心啊。但难道她不知道女人有些不能越过的边界吗？假如男人让女人去做100件事，女人顶多做其中的10件事就好了。因为男人不理解一些很实际的细节啊！……过去的好女人从不会去做这些花哨的事啊……也正是因为这样，大家庭才得以和睦相处啊……但现在所有事情都不一样了！要是拉纳德先生暗示一件事，拉巴芭就会去做三件事！那我们还能有什么自尊呢？我们该如何忍受这一切？”

这些声音，加上民族主义的自相矛盾的主题、家族式的意识形态，以及妇女对男人的抗争，让我们看到了殖民时期印度的私人生活和资产阶级个人主义的冲突。但是历史学家却通过“否定的否定”这样的推理方式，没有给这样一个声音以合理的地位。这样的对资产阶级私人生活作为历史主体的否定，很多历史学家都意识到，但是他们认为要把印度历史写成跟其他的反映普世价值（亦即在欧洲文艺复兴之后提出的公民权、民族国家、人性解放等价值）的历史一样，后者的重要性要更大。但是，恰恰是公民在历史的发展过程中发声了。只要确实有这样的事情发生，我的虚拟的欧洲就会重新出现，笼罩在我的故事周围。正如梅根·莫里斯（Meaghan Morris）在谈论她的澳洲背景时所说，“现代是一段**已经为人所知的历史，发生在某个角落，**将会就地被复制，不管是人为的还是其他方式。”于是我们就只能复制出“积极的非原创性项目”[46]。

五

但是这些谚语的“起源”——虽然我知道这个词本身是一个坏词——却经历了许多波折，而且所有这些都不是在现代发生的。即使你不是信奉父系宗族的传统，你依然可以看到被神圣化的以及家族式的家庭脉络是印度民族主义文化政治的最重要的元素。在对抗英国殖民统治的时期，人们就是在歌曲、诗篇以及其他民族动员的方式中广泛的使用这一谚语，使得“印度人”产生出一种一体感，进而产生出主体的意识，去对抗来自英国的占领。我想可以用“印度之父”甘地的一个故事来说明这样一波文化潮流至于“印度”民族认同的意义。

这个故事发生在1946年，那一年在印度教徒与穆斯林教徒之间因为即将发生的由一国分裂为印度和巴基斯坦两国而出现严重的骚乱。当时甘地就在加尔各答，面对民众的暴乱，甘地选择了绝食。以下就是印度的知识分子对于这一事件的回忆：

男人晚上回到家里会发现家里的女人饭已经帮他们把饭做好了，但人们很快发现，家里的女人一整天都没有吃。她们显然不觉得饥饿。假如你进一步问她们的话，她们会说：甘地都在为他们自己的罪而挨饿，我们又怎么能心甘情愿的吃下去？饭馆和游乐中心也显得非常冷清，有些店还主动关门了……情感的神经终于恢复了，毕竟人们也感到苦楚了……甘地知道什么时候该开始赎罪的过程了[47]。

我们不需字对字的相信上面的描述，但是字里行间所透露出来的社区品质却是十分清晰的。用斯皮瓦克（Spivak）的话来说，“它使得关联国家的情感与关联社区的情感”得以混合起来[48]。

殖民时期的印度就充满了许多这样的例子：印度人通过一些反历史反现代的集体记忆，为他们自身取得了主体性，而这些行为通常都是在“现代”机构有时甚至是民族主义鼓吹的现代化大背景下发生的[49]。这并不是要否认印度人也有我们所说的“历史感”（或者用彼得·布克的话来说，就是“对过去的文艺复兴”），而是要强调，在同一历史时期，也有相反的潮流。在那个殖民时期的印度，各种各样的斗争都在 发生，而对过去的反历史构建则往往可以为人们构筑出非常有力的集体记忆[50]。

也正是在这样一种双重绑定之下，“印度”历史得以充分的展现自我。一方面，它同时是现代性的主体和客体，因为它就是想象中的“印度人民”的历史，虽然这一群体总是会一分为二——走向现代化的精英阶层以及还未走向现代化的农民阶层。正是因为有这样的分裂，所以“印度人民”反映的是民族国家的整体声音，这一整体声音的理论主体只能是一个虚幻的“欧洲”。这一“欧洲”是通过殖民主义者以及民族主义者对被殖民者的叙说而被构建起来的。“印度人”可以表现自我的方式就是霍米·巴巴所说的“模仿型”的[51]。即使是在最严谨的社会主义或民族主义者的描述下，印度历史都不过是现代“欧洲”历史的模拟，并且肯定是象征着欠缺和失败。转型叙述总是会让人感到“悲伤的不完整”。

而另一方面，在模拟之外也有一些回旋的空间。于是在“印度”历史这一课题下，要展现出“印度”的“不一样”以及“原创性”，就会用得上反历史的记忆以及来自庶民阶层的历史记录。于是，农民 / 工人阶层对“神秘的”王国的构建以及“神秘的”过去 / 将来的构建都可以在那些“印度”历史的文章里找到一席之地，但这些人的声音却又正是被那些非神权的、线性的“历史”记述方式所压制的。所以，这些反历史、反现代的主体就不能为自己找到一套理论，因为这是在传统大学的知识体系里所不接纳的，虽然传统的体系也承认被记录了其存在。就像斯皮瓦克笔下的“庶民”，他们只能被转型叙述代言（或者像是人类学家笔下的农民那样，只有可能是在人类学家笔下的文字里以引述的方式出现），而后者总是会偏袒现代化一面（也就是“欧洲”）的[52]。

只要是大学传统划定的“历史”的话语范围内去讨论，就不可能走出“历史”与公民的现代性叙述、“历史”与资产阶级公共私人生活以及“历史”与民族国家这几个深层冲突。在传统的知识体系里，“历史”必然是会跟民族国家走在一起的，只要去看看人们怎么教历史、怎么招募历史教师以及历史系的宣传和出版，就明白这一点。虽然也曾有个别的历史学家大胆的走出这个牢笼，但是整一套的体系还是存活了下来。我们不妨问一问：为什么在今天的现代国家当中，历史都被当成是必修课程？这里有些国家在 18 世纪之前根本就没有历史课啊？为什么现在全世界所有的小孩都必须学习“历史”，而实际上这样的要求既非天生亦非源自远古？[53]不需太多的思索，我们可以得出这样的结论，即这是欧洲殖民主义以及第三世界国家民族主义协力催生出来的产物：他们让人们相信，民族国家是最值得追求的政治社群方式。民族国家可以通过各种手段来强化这一意识。而大学也往往成为这一进程的帮凶（虽然也有一些大学是持批判立场）。“经济学”以及“历史”是资产阶级崛起（以及后来的蔓延）带给世界的两大机构贡献——资本主义式的生产方式以及民族国家（“历史”在给公民说话）[54]。哪怕是一个带批判眼光的历史学家，也只能在此概念基础上进行研究。也就是说，历史学家只能在承认民族国家（公民权以及现代性）的合理性基础上进行探索。而所有这些都会把我们带到欧洲“现代”政治哲学上——甚至也包括更“实用”的经济学，而后者理论上是根源于18世纪欧洲的伦理学[55]——第三世界国家的历史学家就只能把欧洲看成是“现代”的发源地，而与此相反，欧洲本土的历史学家则没有这样的思想包袱。这就是我在文章开头提到的非西方国家的历史学带有庶民色彩的缘由。

但是，另一方面，当我们所有人都是在“欧洲”的历史思维下进行研究时，那些非欧洲的研究者因为可以获得本土化的档案，这就使得我们可以搭建一种嫁接大都会历史以及庶民历史的桥梁。我们不妨将此称作地方化欧洲。很显然，这里的“欧洲”是一个已经被殖民者以及民族主义者联合构建起来的全球图景了。从哲学上来讲，这一项目必须建立在对自由主义（例如对公民权、现代国家以及资产阶级隐私的官僚构建，这些都是由古典政治哲学诞生出来的）的严正批判以及超越的基础上，这样的一个基础也是后期的马克思主义、后结构主义以及女权主义都有所重合的地方。我特别为卡罗尔·帕特曼的在她所写的《性契约》一书里的这一大胆的宣言而感到振奋——现代个体的产生，实际上就是构建于父系思想之上[56]。

六

地方化“欧洲”（provincializing Europe）的项目针对的是一段未曾发生的历史，因此我只能以一种推测的方式来叙述。为了避免产生误解，我得首先声明它不是什么，而后再做深入的解释。

首先，它不是要以一种简单化的方式直接否认现代化，自由的理念，普世的价值，科学，理性、伟大的叙事，更不是要渴望一统所有的理论解释的框架。詹明信（Fredric Jameson）最近也曾提醒过我们说，“某种哲学上的大一统概念化”以及“政治上的极权实践”二者之间的相辅相成是非常可怕的[57]。而处于二者之间的就是历史，而历史往往就充满了各种彼此对立、复杂而且交叉重叠 的斗争，这些斗争的结果往往也是不可预估的，哪怕是事后在知道相关的规律之后进行回顾，也很难设想。这样的斗争包括威胁（有拥护和反对现代性的）——身体上的、机构上的或象征式的暴力，通常会带有一些热切的理想主义，正是这样的暴力在构建意义以及创建掌握真理的政权的过程中发挥了决定性的作用，因为后者可以决定哪一个普世的价值可以获得支持。即使是在象牙塔的学者，也难免受到这样的斗争的冲击，因为我们也不能完全脱离整个社会的知识机构。

正因如此，“地方化欧洲”的项目也不能成为一个“文化相对主义”的项目。不能因为理性 / 科学 / 普世价值等让欧洲体现出其现代性的特质是某些文化所特有的，换言之，是欧洲特有的。不是说启蒙时期的理性主义总是坏的，而是希望现在我们可以通过追寻历史的轨迹去记录这样的“理性”是如何发生的，因为这样的过程并非一眼就可以看得出来的，是有人将其凸现出来的。假如我们说一个国家的官方语言是靠军队支撑起来的，那么关于“**现代性**”的叙述，也可以有同样的说法。人们不管在什么地方，谈及现代性，都会指向“欧洲”的某一块，因为人们相信那里是现代化的主要起源。

但是，欧洲和“西方”一样，也纯粹是想象的个体，但这并不减低它的魅力或影响。地方化“欧洲”的项目还需要包含其他一些步骤：第一，欧洲在历史上把“现代化”与其自身划上了等号，这个本身就是全球历史的一部分，而且这一历史进程是欧洲殖民史不可分割的一部分；第二，把欧洲与“现代性”划等号，这不仅仅是欧洲人的行为，第三世界国家的民族主义者也同样热衷于追捧现代化潮流，他们扮演了几乎同等重要的角色。这不是说要忽视民族主义在发展初期的反帝国运动，我只是想说明，“欧洲”省际化不能仅仅是欧洲人或民族主义者或返祖主义者的项目。

要摆脱充满诸如“权利”、“公民权”、“民族国家”、“公共”和“私有”等历史的纠葛——要知道历史是一种被国家机构强制的集体记忆——就不得不将“印度”问题化，同时也要把欧洲进行细致的解剖。

我希望可以把那些含糊不清、矛盾冲突、暴力、悲剧以及讽刺写进历史。来自资产阶级对于平等、公民权以及自身权利的索求，在很大程度上也帮助了那些边缘群体的抗争。这样的认知对于“庶民研究”是必不可少的。在那些明里暗里赞颂现代国家之诞生以及公民权的历史叙述里，往往是对话语策略的赞颂胜于对反抗以及暴力的描述，但是后者与前者一样重要。而假如你要找到最明显的讽刺图景——也就是建立于非民主基础上的“民主”——看看现代医学、公共卫生、个人卫生的发展历史就明白了。整一个叙述就是把现代的人体放在了公共与私有的交叉点上（而且受到国家的管理和界定）。

而这样的话语之所以获得胜利，一直都是因为它有国家军队的支撑。之所以说是“一直”，是因为这样的强制是根源性的（历史性的），也是具传染性和日常性的。关于暴力的根源性，大卫·阿诺德在最近一篇关于印度监狱的文章里写到了很好的例子。殖民时期的印度监狱对于早期医疗以及饮食方面的研究具有不可或缺的意义，因为只有在监狱，当时的那些具有现代化意识的研究者才能找到可供研究的人体[58]。而关于在国家以及现代化旗号下的压迫，一个时间较近的例子是1970年代的消灭天花斗争。两位参与此项目的美国医生（其中一人应当是有“印度”背景），他们在描述在印度比哈尔邦的Ho部落进行手术的情况：

在一个平静的印度之夜，一位入侵者闯进了这个简陋的草屋。他是政府派来的疫苗接种师，是奉命来强制接种的。拉希米·辛格惊醒了，她尖叫着，在地上爬要躲起来。他丈夫从床上跳起来，拿起一把斧头，一直把那位入侵者追到院子里。外面的一班医生和警察很快就制服了莫汉·辛格．人们把他按在地上，第二位接种师就把天花疫苗注视到他手臂上。莫汉·辛格是Ho部落的首领，时年40岁。接种时他像蛇一样来回摆动，使得伤口出血。政府的官员按住他，直到疫苗完全注射完毕……这两位警察回绝了他，其余的入侵者则制服了整一户人家，逐一完成了接种。拉希米紧紧的咬住了医生的手，但还是没有办法。”[59]

也就是说，伴随着理想主义的总是有暴力。这一文章的题目则反映出了这样一种行为的暴力性以及人性。这个题目是这样写的：“一支撒玛利亚人(指圣经中的Good Samiritans典故)如何把天花赶出地球”。

那些希望将虚拟的欧洲从中心铲除的历史——也就是目前几乎所有历史的中心——就需要很认真的去考量这一暴力与理想主义之间的关系。正是在这一过程中，公民权以及现代性得以回到了“历史”这个天然的家。这里我要提出与理查德·罗蒂、哈贝马斯对话时完全相反的观点。罗蒂批评哈贝马斯说，“现代哲学就是民主社会走向自我认同的重要组成部分。”[60] 罗蒂的观点跟很多欧洲主义者的观点一样，他们认为自己可以为那些“民主社会”代言，以为这些社会的历史本身是独成一体的，或者说西方的自我认知是在其疆域内自然会发生的事情。至少洛蒂没有看到“殖民戏剧”（不管是对内还是对外的）——在这样的地方，“自由”总是和“文明”“进步”“发展”等挂钩在一起的——对于这样的认同所起到的作用。于是我认为，我们需要重新去审视那些评定现代国家及其架构的理念，以使得我们可以最后回归到政治哲学。我们希望印度民间商人的钱可以最终回到他们口袋中。这是同样的道理。而且很显然，世界也不得不开始重视印度卢比了。

最后，因为在传统的大学知识框架里，欧洲是不能被地方化的。所以这一项目本身是不可能完成的。因为我们目前的历史是由一种充满绝望情绪的政治所左右的。现在大家应当明白，这不是要呼唤文化相对主义或追寻返祖、土著历史。也不是要简单的反对现代历史，因为在目前很多国家，这么做就等同于政治上的自杀。我希望看到的一种历史是可以看得到其压迫策略和过程的历史。在现代国家形成的过程中，它与公民权的追求同时塑造了历史，塑造了现代国家里关于和谐共处的诸多的可能性。而绝望的政治又要求这样的历史将为何这样的困境是不可避免的这一原因讲述清楚。这将会是一个尝试去做不可能之事的历史：它要从对自身的死亡那里得到启示，从文化以及言语的转译中找到一些全人类共有的元素。进而把我们引向一个从根本上更为多元的图景。这在传统的大学知识体系下是不可能的，我已经讲过，因为学术的国际化离不开现代欧洲所创造出来的全球化。所以说，地方化欧洲实际上是希望将现代视为一个必然的相互竞争的过程。要超越公民权这一话语所带来的区别对待，从梦想的过去以及未来中汲取到一种共同的记忆，这样的记忆既非由礼教亦非由“传统”与“现代”相互冲突而产生出的梦魇。当然没有任何的基础设施可以容纳这样的梦，但是只要我们一提到历史转折时期的公民权以及民族国家时，都必然会提到这样的梦。

（翻译：陈恒）

有很多来自美国和澳洲的读者读过我的文章并且提出了批评意见，我对此表示感激。要感谢的人太多了，这里列出的一些人我觉得是最需要被感谢的：汤马斯·拉逵尔，本尼迪克特·安德森，阿俊·阿帕杜来，大卫·阿诺德，马乔瑞·比勒，帕沙·查特吉，拿塔里·戴维斯，尼古拉斯·迪克斯，西蒙·杜灵，约翰·福斯特，拉纳吉特·古哈，吉那特·霍恩，马丁·杰，珍妮·李，大卫·罗德，菲奥那·尼科，盖安能德拉·潘德，克莱格·雷诺斯，琼·斯各特以及盖亚特里·斯皮瓦克。还要特别的感谢克利斯托弗·希里，她不但为我提供了智力上的分享，还帮我把这篇文章打出来。

注释：

1 拉纳吉特·古哈，佳娅特里·查卡拉沃蒂·斯皮瓦克编，《庶民研究选集》（*Selected Subaltern Studies*），纽约，1988 年；罗那德·因登（Ronald Inden），“东方主义对印度的建构”(Orientalist Constructions of India)，选自《当代亚洲研究》(*Modern Asian Studies*)，第 20 期，no.3，1986 年，第 445 页。

2 我从让·鲍德利亚那里学到了“虚拟”这个词，[请参考他写的《拟仿》(*Simulations*)，纽约，1983 年]，但是我这里的用法与他的用法不一样。

3 林达·哈钦，《后现代主义的政治》，伦敦，1989 年，第 65 页。

4 埃德蒙德·胡塞尔（Edmund Husserl），《欧洲科学以及超验哲学的危机》（*The Crisis of European Sciences and Transcendental Philosophy*），大卫·卡尔(David Carr)译，埃文斯顿，1970 年，281-285 页；另见威廉·海尔伯法斯（Wilhelm Halbfass），《印度与欧洲：一次理解的尝试》（*India and Europe: An Essay in Understanding*），纽约，1988 年，167-168 页。

5 见马克思《政治经济学批判大纲》，马丁·尼古拉斯（Martin Nicholas）翻译，英国哈蒙斯华兹，1973 年，469-512 页；以及马克思《资本论》三卷册，莫斯科，1971 年，第三卷，593-613 页。

6 参见迪佩什·查卡拉巴提，《孟加拉工人阶级历史的重新思考：1890-1940》（*Rethinking Working-Class History: Bengal, 1890-1940*），新泽西州普林斯顿，1989 年，第 7 章。

7 马克思，《资本论》，第一卷，第 60 页。

8 马克思，《政治经济学批判大纲》，第 105 页。

9 参见查卡拉巴提，《孟加拉工人阶级历史的重新思考》，第 7 章。

10 苏米特·萨卡尔，《现代印度：1885—1947 年》(*Modern India, 1885-1947*)，德里，1985 年，第 1 章。

11 古哈和斯皮瓦克，《庶民研究选集》，第 43 页。这里引用的是古哈的话。但我相信它所代表的是一种历史责任，这是所有庶民研究的成员都认同的。

12 亚历山大·道尔，《印度斯坦历史》（*History of Hindostan*），3 卷本，伦敦，1812-1816 年，卷首词，第 1 卷。

13 参见 L·T·霍布豪斯（L. T. Hobhouse），《自由主义》（*Liberalism*），纽约，1964 年，26-27 页。

14 尼拉德·C·乔杜里（Nirad C. Chaudhuri），《一位不知名的印度人的自传》（*The Autobiography of an Unknown Indian*），纽约，1989 年，卷首词。

15 帕沙·查特吉，《民族主义思潮与殖民世界：一种推论话语？》（*Nationalist Thought and the Colonial World: A Derivative Discourse?*），伦敦，1986 年。

16 （*Mudhusudan rachanabali*）（孟加拉文），加尔各答，1965 年，第 449 页；另见乔金度朗那斯·巴苏（Jogindranath Basu），（*Michael Madhusudan Datter jibancharit*）（孟加拉文），加尔各答，1978 年，第 86 页。

17 经过与马乔瑞·利文逊（Marjorie Levinson）和大卫·本尼特（David Bennett）的讨论，我对于此诗的理解有了大大的提升。

18 我并不是说所有这些种类都会伴随着资产阶级个人主义的兴起而兴起。参见拿塔里·西蒙·戴维斯（Natalie Zemon Davis），"名声与秘密：莱昂·摩德纳的早期自传"（Fame and Secrecy: Leon Modena's Lqe as an Early Modern Autobiography），《历史与理论》（*History and Theory*）第 27 期，1988 年，103-118 页；以及戴维斯，"16 世纪法国的边界以及自我感觉"（Boundaries and Sense of Self in Sixteenth-Century France），收于汤马斯·C·赫勒（Thomas C. Heller）等编辑的《重构个人主义：西方思想里的自主、个体以及自我》（*Reconstructing Individualism: Autonomy, Individuality, and the Self in Western Thought*），加州斯坦福，1986 年，53-63 页。另外还可以参考菲利普·勒琼（Philippe Lejeune），《论自传》（*On Autobiography*），凯瑟琳·拉尔里（Katherine Leary）译，明尼阿波利斯，1989 年，163-184 页。

19 参见查特吉所著《民族主义思潮》关于尼赫鲁的章节。

20 甘地，《印度自治》(*Hindswaraj*)，1909 年，收于《圣雄甘地全集》，第 10 卷，阿默达巴德，1963 年，第 15 页。

21 参见高里·维斯凡那森（Gauri Visvanathan），《征服的面具：文学研究与英国在印度的统治》(*Masks of Conquest: Literary Studies and British Rule in India*)，伦敦，1989 年，128-141 页。

22 拉纳吉特·古哈（Ranajit Guha），《印度殖民时期农民起义概况》（*Elementary Aspects of Peasant Insurgency in Colonial India*），德里，1983 年，第 2 章。

23 威廉·E·科诺里（William E. Connolly），《政治理论与现代性》（*Political Theory and Modernity*），牛津，1989 年；另见大卫·本尼特，《后现代与视角：历史终结的观察方法》（*Postmodernism and Vision: Ways of Seeing (at) the End of History*），即将出版。

24 哈贝马斯，《公共空间的结构转换：资产阶级社会阶层考察》（*The Structural Transformation of the Public Sphere: An Inquiry into a Category of Bourgeois Society*），麻省剑桥，1989 年，第 49 页。

25 参见苏米特·萨卡尔，"社会历史：困境与可能"（Social History: Predicament and Possibilities），伊卡波·可汗（Iqbal Khan）编，《印度巴基斯坦新视角：经济、政治、文学文选》（*Fresh Perspective on India and Pakistan: Essays on Economics, Politics, and Culture*），牛津，1985 年，256-274 页。

26 鉴于空间有限，这里我就不展开论述，但还是希望在其他地方可以更详细的探讨。另外我想指出，它主要是指 1850 年到 1910 年间出版的自传。到 20 世纪妇女进入公共空间之后，她们的自述则呈现更多的风格。

27 尼拉德·C·乔杜里，《您的贵手，伟大的无政府！：印度 1921-1952》（*Thy Hand, Great Anarch!: India, 1921-1952*），伦敦，1987 年，350-51 页。

28 参见马克思，"论犹太问题"（On the Jewish Question），见于《早期著述》（*Early Writings*），英国哈蒙德斯华兹，1975 年，215-222 页。

29 要了解后面发生了什么事情，请看我写的“殖民统治与家庭秩序”（Colonial Rule and the Domestic Order），将在《庶民研究》第8期发表。

30 梅瑞迪斯·波兹维克（Meredith Borthwick），《孟加拉女性角色变迁：1849-1905》（*The Changing Role of Women in Bengal, 1849-1905*），新泽西普林斯顿，1984年；古兰·莫什得（Ghulam Murshid），《孟加拉女性对现代化的态度：1849-1905》（*Reluctant Debutante: Response of Bengali Women to Modernisation, 1849-1905*），1983年。关于可视化的历史，可以看陆辰·费弗尔（Lucien Febvre）写的“文明：一个词的演化和一组概念的演化”（Civilisation: Evolution of a Word and a Group of Ideas），收于彼得·布克思（Peter Burke）编，《新历史：费弗尔的笔记》（*A New Kind of History: From the Writings of Febvre*），K·富尔卡（K. Folca）译，伦敦，1973年，219-257页。感谢彼得·沙林（Peter Sahlins）为我提供了这一线索。

31 詹姆斯·密尔（James Mill），《英属印度历史》（*The History of British India*），第1卷，见H·H·威尔逊（H. H. Wilson）编，伦敦，1840年，309-310页。

32 波兹维克，《孟加拉女性角色变迁》。

33 这一推断的哲学来源是黑格尔的《法哲学原理》，T·M·克诺思（T.M. Knox）译，牛津，1967年，110-122页。另见琼娜·霍奇（Joanna Hodge），“妇女与黑格尔国家”（*Women and the Hegelian State*），收录于伊伦·肯尼迪（Ellen Kennedy）和苏珊·孟德斯（Susan Mendus）编，《西方哲学中的妇女》（*Women in Western Philosophy*），英国布来顿，1987年，127-158页；西蒙·杜灵（Simon During），《卢梭后裔：原始主义、浪漫主义以及其他现代与非现代的关系》（*Rousseau's Heirs: Primitivism, Romance, and Other Relations Between the Modern and the Nonmodern*），即将出版；琼·B·兰德斯（Joan B. Landes），《法国革命时期的妇女与公共空间》（*Women and the Public Sphere in the Age of the French Revolution*），纽约伊萨卡，1988年；玛丽·瑞安（Mary Ryan），《公共空间里的妇女：旗帜与选票：1825-1880》（*Women in Public: Between Banners and Ballots, 1825-1880*），巴尔的摩，1990年。

34 无名氏，《妇女教育》（*Streesiksha*），第 1 卷，加尔各答，1877 年，28-29 页。

35 关于这一论述，我将在即将发表的“开放的公共空间：垃圾、现代性以及印度”（Open Space/Public Place: Garbage, Modernity, and India）里有所阐述。

36 迪那班独·兰卡那巴里（Dinabandhu racanabali）编，《卡什特拉·古塔》（*Kshetra Gupta*），加尔各答，1981 年，第 138 页。

37 波兹维克，《孟加拉女性角色变迁》，第 105 页。

38 我在“殖民统治与家庭秩序”一文里有更详尽的讨论。

39 英迪拉·戴维，《女性发声》（*Narir ukti*），加尔各答，1920 年，卷首词。

40 迪恩那斯·班迪奥帕丫丫（Deenanath Bandyopadhyaya），（*Nanabishayak prabandha*），加尔各答，1887 年，30-31 页。要了解关于奴役以及自由这样的词汇在英属印度殖民时期的使用情况详细记录，请看赛扬·普拉卡什（Cyan Prakash），《捆绑的历史：印度殖民时期的劳务服务体系研究》（*Bonded Histories: Genealogies of Labor Servitude in Colonial India*），剑桥，1990 年。

41 彼得·布克（Peter Burke），《关于过去的文艺复兴联想》（*The Renaissance Sense of the Past*），伦敦，1970 年。

42 比什舒克（钱德拉塞卡·森）（Bikshuk [Chandrasekhar Sen]），（*Ki holo!*），加尔各答，1876 年，第 77 页。

43 大卫·金斯利（David Kinsley），《印度诸神：印度教传统里的神圣女性形象》（*Hindu Goddesses: Visions of the Divine Feminine in the Hindu Religious Tradition*），伯克莱，1988 年，19-31 页；曼诺莫汗·巴苏（Manomohan Basu），（*Hindu acar byabahar*），加尔各答，1873 年，第 60 页；H·D·巴塔查雅（H. D. Bhattacharya），“少数派的宗教团体”，收于 R·C·马俊达（R. C. Majumdar）编，《印度人民的历史与文化：帝国统一时期》（*The History and Culture of the Indian People: The Age of Imperial Unity*），第 2 卷，孟买，1951 年，469-471 页；尤潘德兰那斯·达乐（Upendranath Dhal），《拉希米神的起源与发展》（*Goddess Lakshmi: Origin and Development*），德里，1978 年。

44 参见查特吉《民族主义思潮与殖民世界：一种推论话语？》里关于班金的章节。

45 《拉那德：他妻子的回忆》(*Ranade: His Wife's Reminiscences*)，库苏马伐提·德什潘德（Kusumavati Deshpande）译，德里，1963 年，第 77 页。

46 米汗·莫里斯（Meaghan Morris），“悉尼塔的转变”（Metamorphoses at Sydney Tower），《新形态》(*New Formations*)，第 11 期，1990 年夏，第 10 页。

47 阿米亚·查卡拉法提（Amiya Chakravarty），引述自比库·帕拉（Bhikhu Parekh），《甘地的政治论述》（*Gandhi's Political Discourse*），伦敦，1989 年，第 163 页。

48 斯皮瓦克，“庶民可以发声吗？”（Can the Subaltern Speak?），见卡瑞·尼尔森（Cary Nelson）和劳伦斯·古罗斯伯（Lawrence Grossberg）编，《马克思主义以及对文化的解释》（*Marxism and the Interpretation of Culture*），伊利诺伊州厄尔巴纳，1988 年，第 277 页。

49 参见《庶民研究》第 1-7 卷，德里，1982-1991 年；以及阿希斯·南迪，《亲密的敌人：殖民统治下自我的丧失与恢复》，德里，1983 年。

50 《庶民研究》，第 1-7 卷，以及古哈《印度殖民时期农民起义概况》。

51 霍米·巴巴（Homi Bhabha），“模仿与人：论殖民话语的含糊性”（Of Mimicry and Man: The Ambivalence of Colonial Discourse），见安妮特·米切尔森（Annette Michelson）等编，《十月：第一个十年：1976-1986》（*October: The First Decade, 1976-1986*），麻省剑桥，1987 年，317-326 页；以及巴巴编，《国家与叙事》（*Nation and Narration*），伦敦，1990 年。

52 斯皮瓦克，《庶民可以发声吗？》，还可以参考斯皮瓦克的一个采访录，发表于《社会学评论》（*Socialist Review*）第 20 期，卷 3，1990 年 7-9 月号，81-98 页。

53 要了解帝国意识形态以及印度殖民时期历史的教授情况，请看拉纳吉特·古哈写的《印度的历史图景：19 世纪的议程及其影响》（*An Indian Historiography of India: A Nineteenth-Century Agenda and Its Implications*），加尔各答，1988 年。

54 我可以说这里的一些言论与盖杨·普拉卡什（Gyan Prakash）以及尼古拉斯·迪克斯（Nicholas Dirks）在其他地方的论说有平行之处。参见盖杨·普拉卡什，“第三世界后东方学历史的撰写：从印度历史视角出发”（Writing Post-Orientalist Histories of the Third World: Perspectives from Indian Historiography），《社会与历史比较研究》（*Comparative Studies in Society and History*），第 32 期，第 2 卷，1990 年 4 月号，383-408 页；尼古拉斯·B·迪克斯，“历史是现代的符号”（History as a Sign of the Modern），《公共文化》（*Public Culture*），第 2 期，1990 年春季号，25-33 页。

55 见阿马蒂亚·库马尔·森（Amartya Kumar Sen），《论伦理学与经济学》（*Of Ethics and Economics*），牛津，1987 年。特萨·莫里斯—铃木（Tessa Morris-Suzuki）的《日本经济思想历史》（*A History of Japanese Economic Thought, 伦敦，1989 年*）也是本主题下很好的读物。我要感谢盖凡·麦科马克（Gavan McCormack），是他把这本书介绍给我。

56 卡罗尔·帕特曼，《性契约》（*The Sexual Contract*），加州斯坦福，1988 年，第 184 页。

57 詹明信（Fredric Jameson），“认知图解”（Cognitive Mapping），见尼尔森和古罗斯伯共同编写的《马克思主义以及对文化的解释》，第 354 页。

58 大卫·阿诺德，“殖民监狱：19 世纪印度的权力、知识以及刑罚学”（The Colonial Prison: Power, Knowledge, and Penology in Nineteenth-Century India），刊发于阿诺德和哈迪曼编辑的《庶民研究》第 8 期。我在一篇孟加拉文的文章中也提到这一题目，见“Sarir, samaj, o rashtra: Oupanibeshik bharate mahamari o janasangskriti”，1988 年。

59 罗沦斯·布利连（Lawrence Brilliant）以及歌里亚·布利连（Girija Brilliant），“致命疾病的死亡”（Death for a Killer Disease），（*Quest*），1978 年 5-6 月合刊。感谢保罗·格林诺（Paul Greenough）为我提供了这一线索。

60 理查德·罗蒂（Richard Rorty），“哈贝马斯与李欧塔论后现代”（Habermas and Lyotard on Postmodernity），见理查德·J·伯恩斯坦（Richard J. Bernstein）编，《哈

贝马斯与现代性》（*Habermas and Modernity*），麻省剑桥，1986 年，第 169 页。

61 要了解更多关于黑格尔在这方面的有趣论断，请看查尔斯·泰勒（Charles Taylor）与帕沙·查特吉之间的通信，刊发于《公共文化》第 3 期，no.1，1990 年。我写的“重新认识工人阶层之历史”（Rethinking Working-Class History）也是希望从更小的层面去切入这一问题。

晚近民主制度中的博物馆

民主的两种模式

在我进入博物馆及其展开的与民主的关系问题——这是我这篇简短的、概述性论文的真正主题——之前，让我简要地介绍我眼中于当代民主政治中并存且时而对撞的两种民主的模式来作为开始。出于简洁和明白的考虑，我将力求保持我的模式（划分）独立且简单。十九世纪和二十世纪早期的民主观念假设了一种对政治的教育学的理解。人生来绝不是政治的，即便在人们认为所有人都有能力或潜能参与政治生活的情况下亦如此。但是人之为人的条件异于人之为政治动物的条件。人们假设，成为一个公民，拥有并行使权利，要求适宜的教育形式。人们认为社会既有高等的又有低等的文化形式。教育提供了公民所需的鉴别能力——进入高等文化的通道。这可能是自我教育，也可能是通过种类正确的经验来进行的教育。然而更为常见的是，人们认为，提供公民能力，是现代社会教育体制的（任务）。大学、博物馆、图书馆、展览和其他类似的组织体承担了这项职责。[1] 这种教育的决定性的一面，是抽象的概念化和理性推理的能力。书变成体现这种设想的关键物。赋予作为教授媒介的书面语的重要性，则显示了此种思维模式给予人类经训练获得的抽象能力的崇高地位。抽象推理使公民能够概念化诸如“阶级”，“公共”或“民族（或国家）”利益这样的想象 / 实体，并能在诸多说法中进行权衡裁量。理性不仅是生活中的争端的程序性方面；它本身就被认为是公共讨论中的一种统一的工具。理性能够帮助我们领会我们的利益并在心智上以正确的优先次序对这些利益进行安排。公共领域不但被想象为潜在地统一且一致的；这样的统一本身就是一种价值。对于马克思主义来说，“阶级”可能是解释和促进这种多个被剥削群体之间的统一的理性关键词。对民族主义者来说，像“民族利益”这样的东西可能是统御一切出自局部利益的分歧的因素。对于自由主义者来说，理性可以导向对所有人的利益的领会。通过教育和理性的辩论来扩大共识的领域被看作强化民族 / 国家生活之构造的方式。

这种对公民权的训导式的理解并非历史。它不是某种我们已留在身后的东西。许多我们制度和个人的行为都基于这种理解。然而二十世纪的大众—民主实践——既在西方也在像印度那样的（非西方）国家——也取决于对政治的非常别样的理解。循着霍米·巴巴对“训导的（pedagogic）”和“述行的（performative）”术语的使用，我们可以把民主政治的第二种模式称作一种“述行的”民主。[2]在这种模式中，民主在根本上并不是一个训导的问题。公民不是在某种教育程序的终端到来或被生产出来的人，而在这种教育程序中学校、大学、图书馆和博物馆都（对公民的产生）进行干预。在这个日益主导自二十世纪六十年代以来民主中的公共生活中的、与公共生活有关的辩论的概念中，人之为人就意味着成为已然政治的存在。诸如“一切都是政治”或“个人就是政治”此类的陈述就是这种观点的反映。一个澳大利亚的例子将说明我对这两种民主模式之间的差别的看法。A · P · 伊尔金（A. P. Elkin）——他于 1934 年至 1956 年任悉尼大学人类学教授——拥护原住民的公民权，但他只支持对这类权利的“一种渐进的授予”。在他看来，只有“开化的”原住民才配拥有公民权。 在我看来，伊尔金，代表的就是第一种模式。然而原住民最终于 1967 年取得了（部分的）公民权，这个决定显然没有反映伊尔金的立场。[4]任何原住民，无论是否受过正式的教育，现在都被看作有资格拥有公民权利的人。这也适用于印度，在取得独立的时候，在一个文盲居多的社会中采取了作为一项公民权利的普选权的决定。这是这样一种全球性趋势的一部分，其开端至少可以追溯到二十世纪二十年代，在对布尔什维主义的恐惧，比如说，引起西方政府在许多国家扩大工人阶级组织和抗议的权利的时候。这些权利的获得在人民一方不再以任何准备性劳作为前提条件。简言之，教育或训导模式的政治跟不上上个世纪世界政治化的脚步。苏联革命，非西方的反殖民的大众民族主义，以及西方大众政治的出现，直到二十世纪五十年代都对此进程影响巨大。接着我们则迎来了二十世纪六十年代的“新”社会运动和反文化运动，以“个人即政治”为口号的第一波女性主义以及在西方民主国家中的多元文化主义和原住民权利政治。消费主义与大众媒体的传播已经是这种对大众民主形式的诉求不可分割的一部分。因为消费大众之兴起及其权利的问题——对资本主义民主国家日益增长的关注——包含了这两种对政治的理解。消费者是训导的主体，教给他们自身的权利是一种经常性的行为。我们有旨在普及这些权利的社团和杂志。但消费者选择或拒绝某种产品（无论出于什么原因）的权利却是一项基本的权利，独立于对这些权利的教育。

可以理解，像大学或博物馆这样的教育机构也未能免于教育和述行性民主之间的紧张关系。二十世纪八十年代所谓的“文化战争”见证了西方学院中的正典遭遇严酷挑战和有力辩护，形形色色的文化相对主义的涌现，在多样性和身份政治上的论调，后现代和后殖民批评的到来，都在这些机构上留下了它们的印记。这些围绕训导式民主与述行性民主的辩论是悬而未决的，但我们却大可以这么说，现在很少——如果有的话——有博物馆或大学想回到十九世纪或二十世纪早期的纯粹的议题并忽视后殖民、原住民和多元文化论者的讨论。它们也不想否认消费主义实践的现实性，而公共机构恰恰坐落在这些实践之中。尽管如此，在特定的机构中，仍然进行着关于这两种用来应对特定情况的政治模式之特定混合的有趣而严格的辩论。其后的决断，不用说，既具原则性，亦是政治的和实际的。它们不为我们面临的两难境地提供任何普世的解决方案，但我把这些争论看作对训导和述行性民主模式之间的张力的一种提醒。这种张力是在晚期民主政体中的我们，在思考那些我们划作“博物馆”的机构的未来时所必须解决的。

和大学一样，博物馆也不得不接受这样的观念，即教育与娱乐并非彼此对立。但博物馆出于我在下面会深入阐释的种种原因，比大学更受这一过程的影响。它们不得不接受这样的建议，即它们的客户有选择权且客户的偏好需要得到满足；教育在很大程度上不得不为自己埋单，国家资金支持必须由捐赠和收入来补充。随之而来的是那些对博物馆在决定收藏什么和展示什么上的权威发起挑战的辩论。博物馆已经被卷入关于过去，及其再现和所有者的辩论，这些辩论常常为所谓身份政治的动因所驱使。最后一点对那些为文化主权诸形式而斗争的人来说一直以来都特别敏感。在世界各地（包括澳大利亚）的原住民已经成功地挑战了这样的观念，即什么东西都能拿来展示给所有人看，或与特定群体对物品的文化使用和占有相比，科学的好奇代表了更大的人类利益。结果，博物馆已经成为在晚期民主政体中关乎过去的种种问题派生出的文化政治的关键场所。

博物馆、民主与经验的政治

我想说，如果训导式的民主模式推崇公民的抽象推理和想象能力的话，那么，述行式的民主模式则把具体化和感官的领域带进视野。而这正是使视觉和其他感官实践在两种模式中互有差异的地方。想想一度以给公民设想和视觉化诸如民族 / 国家之观念那样抽象事物的能力为宗旨的教育吧。当然有视觉教具：地图、雕塑和其他民族统一体的影像。但像历史、地理、政治学和人类学这样的中学和大学学科使人有能力去思考民族 / 国家和社群的方式，是通过开发学生视觉化抽象的技能。我依然清晰记得，1973 年，一位来自加尔各答附近 24 区乡村的不识字的农村女孩，在陪我表哥、她的家人和我自己一同乘汽车从德里到加尔各答途中问我的一个问题。她是我表哥的一个家仆，至今她已经在德里生活了许多年并接触到了电视和电影。然而，离开德里不过几里，她的好奇心就被不熟悉的环境激发起来，问我，“告诉我，迪佩什达（我哥哥，迪佩什），克什米尔是 24 区的一部分么？”我们都笑她对印度地理的无知，但这事也告诉我一个人的地理想象在多大程度上是一个教育和培训个人——用地图这样的工具——来视觉化像民族 / 国家那样完全不可感知的实体方面的问题。

在训导式的民主模式中，公民权基于理性推理的能力。人们假定这种能力如同所有信息必须经过的处理机那样高高在上。仿佛训导模式推崇大脑胜过其他感官。过去博物馆会收集和并置那些就它们在世界范围内的自然 / 文化分布而言从来都不在一起的那些东西。动物园之于动物、图书馆之于书也是如此。所有这些安排都会给概念或分析以超越生活（the lived）的特权。可以说，动物园使一个（物种的）目录册活灵活现。博物馆和档案馆——都是为保存过去的遗物而设的现代机构——在其起源之时，原则上是相近的。就像博物馆馆长忽视展品的感官方面那样，在其学科传统中受过训练的历史学家也很少把其研究对象触觉的或感官的一面纳入他们的叙事。古代脆弱的文献在他们的手上破碎的经验，古旧的报纸的味道，过去书写风格引起的眼睛的负担，档案中的尘土可能引起的过敏——简言之，还有使所谓过去的遗物成为当下生活的一部分的一切——都被放到了一边，目的是为了使过去出现在与当下明确的距离之中。为什么在分析的工作中感觉要被贬低到背景的层次呢？因为，这种思考方式假定，只有通过分析性的推理，人们才能触及更深层次的、普遍的和不显而易见的关于社会的“真理”，无论它们是什么——阶级、经济力量，还是自然法则。那些仅仅是感知层面、并不从属于理性的东西——从这个意义上说还是生活经验的一部分——只能让我们获得局部和特殊的（认识）。

我们可以说，分析总是想要使“经验”或“生活”成为其附庸。[5]然而经验的领域越来越多地强调自己在学院历史学或人类学中的地位——每当这些学科尝试对民主的压力作出回应。但这并不总是带来令人高兴的结果。二十世纪六七十年代的历史学家摸索“口述史”，假定人们诉说的经历将会让文献档案馆里的故事更加生动丰满，从而在不挑战历史学科基本戒律的前提下使学科民主化。然而，他们却发现自己置身于记忆的土地，而这些记忆总在模糊对历史学分析和客观性来说关键的、过去与当下之间的区别。[6]在记忆的领域和学院历史学之间存在一种学科的不和谐。同样，人类学家也被迫与种种从对分析的传统从属关系之中释放生活和经验的策略进行奋斗，但结果毁誉参半。理由不难寻找：与学院学科联姻的政治想象属于我说的第一种民主模式：公民权作为抽象推理的能力。确实，没有这样的推理，社会科学的批判—政治的刀锋就会受挫。怎么可能用其他的方式把像资本、社会结构和工具理性等这样不显而易见的实体视觉化为具体而真实的事物呢?而如果没有这些范畴的话，人们怎样阐发对社会关系的现代批判?

博物馆作为人们无需专门资格即可进入的公共场所，一直以来都更受到大众民主的压力，并不得不更为直接地应对经验的问题。它们因此也就不得不对质疑假定的分析高于生活的首要性的政治更为敏感。在著名的论文“论收藏艺术与文化”（On Collecting Art and Culture）中，人类学家詹姆士·克利福德（James Clifford）为此给出了一个来自巴黎人类博物馆生活的早期的实例。他援引了安·维达尔—法尔杜利（Anne Vitart-Fardoulis，一位博物馆馆长）——于1986年发表的一篇论文。维达尔—法尔多莉描述了一天一位美洲原著民男子是如何走进博物馆并突然，通过以个人和私密的方式谈论“一张著名的绘满复杂图画的动物毛皮”，对分析相对生活的优越性发起挑战的:

与水牛比尔（Buffalo Bill）一道来到巴黎的一位印第安人的子孙，搜寻他的祖父在马戏团倒闭的时候被迫为筹集他回国的旅费而卖掉的那件（彩绘的毛皮）长袍。我给他出示了我们收藏的所有长袍，他在其中一件长袍前停了下来。他一边控制自己的感情，一边讲。他告诉我们这个发结、那个图案的意义，为什么要用这个颜色，那根羽毛的意义……这件衣服，先前美丽而有趣，而今则被动而冷漠，渐渐地变成……（一个）通过某个并非**观察和分析它而是经验**（lived）此客体对象而且此客体/对象也为之而活（lived）的人的沉思，对一个活生生的时刻的积极的见证。这件长袍事实上是不是他祖父的，已经无所谓了。[7]

我不必提醒读者十九世纪这位美洲原著民男子也可以走进一家博物馆并说出这些相同的话，但在那个时候没人会注意他说了些什么。为什么我们现在听见他说话了？因为身份政治——（关于）谁能为谁而说话的问题——不管你喜不喜欢已经成为自由民主国家文化政治的一部分。我们的注意力越是转向先前在西方内部的“被殖民者”，反殖民的主题和问题也就越是标记着自由民主国家在多元文化主义上的努力。殖民主义和殖民知识的历史表明，社会科学的普遍性的和人文主义的分析框架是如何一度被用来分类、控制并迫使西方（范畴）内外的被殖民者服从。[8]也正是同一个过程，导致被殖民者的前殖民的知识体系如今过着被征服的生活，被贬低至据说是狭隘和非理论的、“经验”的领域。恰与这种知识的政治相反，历史上受压迫的等级不时地发出这样的呼声，“和你的档案下地狱吧，我们有经验！”[9]

在是自身对经验的政治开放的同时，博物馆逐渐地远离档案馆，那个它们曾与之共享知识范式的现代机构。因为经验的政治

图 1：南非开普敦第六区博物馆“深挖”展览中的理发店装置。
摄影：哈吉拉·以扫（Haajirah Esau），由第六区博物馆提供

把我们导向感觉和具体化的领域。抽象推理的能力绝无可能实现这一点。它（后者）使我们远离感官，它训练我们对感觉产生出来的关于世界的明证保持怀疑。而另一方面，大学教育能够训练我们，正如我已经说过的那样，把那些对自然的眼睛（肉眼）来说的不可见的东西视觉化为具体的实在。但它对一种具体化的历史主体说话（且谈论这种具体化的历史主体），在我们从这个角度来认识世界的时候这是一个我们个人地被要求占据的立场。然而，今天的博物馆，却持续地使自己向这种具体化和经验开放。它提供的“经验”和抽象一样多。而这，就是直接属于我谈到的第二种民主模式的一部分。

让我们用南非开普敦第六区博物馆的例子来简要地说明这点。许多读者将会知道，第六区是开普敦城一个著名的“混合”社区，严格地说，在 1966 年至 1984 年间被清除并变成白人区。一夜之间成千上万的人失去了他们的住所。家庭和邻里被撕裂分散。博物馆从那场无畏地挑战这个不民主的残酷法令的抗议运动中有机地生长起来。从 1994 年开始，博物馆就发展成了一个为社群记忆的场所，不是对一段死去的过去表示伤怀的纪念碑，而是作为在后种族隔离时代的南非反抗种族主义斗争的一部分的一段活生生的记忆的，怀旧的纪念碑。年长一些的居民和他们的孩子为吸收影响到他们当下的斗争的记忆而参观博物馆。博物馆也做出了特别的努力，来纪念社区的各个街道。这是从一个到博物馆的参观

图 2：第六区博物馆外部，由第六区博物馆提供

者的角度来实现的见证的一部分，它表明铭记的逻辑，异于历史之逻辑，是如何势不可挡地导向感官和具体化的领域：

我孩提时在海角的街道如一个保存完好的清晰骨架上的骨头般幸存了下来。在参观这里的时候，我的记忆奔涌而出，我意识到，这种记忆行动可以比拟为观看视频——不过是以反向的运动……在骨骼周围长出了生存所需的器官，有时还有血肉……但记忆的过程是经过过滤且有纹理的，把彼时和现时的不同阶段纠缠在一起。它在对某种新旧交错的（old-new）事物的召唤中，而不是在一度在那里存在的“血肉”中达到顶点。这个过程同时又是如此地私密而脱离于我们的把握……我们沿着街道行走，把它们和家、学校以及商店的街灯联系起来。在我重复做的一个几近梦魇的梦里，沿着通往学校的主干道，我在令人恶心的恐惧中，提着沉重的手提箱，开始了我的旅途……而记忆进一步绽出；烧灼的人行道、海鸥的尖叫以及低吼的雾号，和泛着黄色泡沫的大海，还有咯吱作响的棕榈树叶；但所有这些中最强的记忆的感觉，是西瓜的味道，从海滨草坪上新割过的草，向附近旅馆、平房和散布的房屋的住户渗透。[10]

你可以在这段引文中看到，最终，记—忆（mem-ory）何以永不能与感觉的领域分离，因为记忆总是具备具体化的元素。我们甚至不能完整地预知这些具体化的记忆。这实际上给经常被轻蔑地称之为“身份政治”的那种东西带来了矛盾的结果。的确，民主国家中多样身份的政治常常引导人民作出把经验与身份相连的站不住脚的主张。比如，人们可能会说——且人们常常这样说——只有某个特定群体的成员才有权利或能力去理解 / 代表这个群体因为他们具有必需的和必不可少的经验。有时，正如我已经说过的那样，知道特定的压迫历史有助于我们同情这些主张。但经验的特质与政治事实上与这样的主张不符。生活的领域最终属于具体化的实在。而经验总是触及这个层面。那么，随着而来的就是，经验并不总是意味着某个界定这经验本身（如此地界定此经验）的主体（或某种认同）。从心理学的意义上说，经验不总是主观的，如果我们所说的心理学指的是在大脑发生的一切的话。[11] 身体也有经验，并记得它们。因此身份政治常常指向这样一个层面，使“身份政治家”让身份看起来固定、不变和基要化的打算无法实现。因为谁能预料身心复合体可能记起或记不起哪些东西呢？因此，经验并不对身份政治开口。

通过对具体化和生活的问题开放，博物馆对某些学院学科置之不理的、现代民主国家中的一些公共构造说话。民主需要知情的公众和公开的辩论。学院的知识模式崇尚那些被认为是大脑进程的信息。这些知识模式边缘化了感觉。民—主（Democ-racies）已经走向多种多样的政治，信息并不简单地一并交由大脑处理；如今信息也处理其他感官——视觉、听觉、嗅觉和触觉。在大众和媒体的民主制度中，具体化的领域在政治上越来越有力。这不是说为传统学院学科所生产的专家和理性变得多余或无关紧要。而是说，它们传统的对具体化与感官的怀疑主义将无助于我们理解为什么记忆与经验——亦即具体化的知识——将在民主国家的政治中扮演的角色，和生产脱离实体的知识的学院学科所渴望扮演的角色同等重要。博物馆和档案馆和历史系相比，走过了为跟上标志晚期民主国家的诸种变化而必须跨越的距离。

(翻译：王立秋)

注释：

1 关于这些问题的讨论，参见西蒙·杜林（Simon During）编，《文化研究读本》（*The Cultural Studies Reader*，伦敦和纽约，Routledge 出版社，1999 年）的导论部分。

2 霍米·巴巴，“撒播：时间，叙事与现代民族国家的边界”（Dissemination: Time, narrative and the margins of the modern nation），见《文化的方位》（*The Location of Culture*），伦敦和纽约，Routledge 出版社，1994 年，139-170 页。

3 “从从游牧到公民权：A·P·伊尔金和原住民的进步”（From Nomadism to Citizenship: A.P.Elkin and Aboriginal Advancement），载尼古拉斯·彼得森（Nicholas Peterson）和威尔·桑德斯（Will Sanders）编：《公民权与澳大利亚原住民：变化的概念与可能性》（*Citizenship and Indigenous Australians: Changing Conceptions and Possibilities*; Cambridge: Cambridge University Press, 1998), pp. 55-76。

4 关于 1967 年澳大利亚公民投票权的复杂与暧昧的讨论，参见贝恩·阿特伍德（Bain Attwood）和安德鲁·马库斯（Andrew Markus）著，“代表问题：1967 年全民公投和公民权”（Representation Matters: The 1967 Referendum and Citizenship），尼古拉斯·彼得森和威尔·桑德斯编，《公民权与澳大利亚原住民：变化的概念与可能性》（*Citizenship and Indigenous Australians: Changing Conceptions and Possibilities*），墨尔本，剑桥大学出版社，1998 年，118-140 页。

5 参见拙著《地方化欧洲：后殖民思想与历史差异》（*Provincializing Europe: Postcolonial Thought and Historical Difference*，新泽西，普林斯顿大学出版社，2000 年）最后一章。

6 改为“经验的明证”（The Evidence of Experience），载《批评探索》（Critical Inquiry），第 17 期，1991 年夏，772-797 页，再生产了——这次是以后结构主义对主体的怀疑——社会分析家对“经验”作为社会现实之导引的有用性的怀疑主义。

7 维达尔—法尔杜利，转引自詹姆士·克利福德，“论收藏艺术与文化”，见其著作《文化的困境：二十世纪的民族学、文学和艺术》（*The Predicament of Culture:*

Twentieth-Century Ethnography, Literature, and Art），麻省剑桥，哈佛大学出版社，1988 年，第 246 页，强调是我加的。

8 伯纳德·科恩（Bernard Cohn）在《殖民主义及其知识形式》（*Colonialism and its Forms of Knowledge*，新泽西，普林斯顿大学出版社，1998 年）中对这里涉及的一些问题作出了经典的论断。

9 我在我的论文“全球化、民主与历史的撤退？”（Globalization, Democratization, and the Evacuation of History?）中对此有更详细的论述，见杰奇·阿萨亚格（Jackie Assayag）和韦罗妮克·拜奈伊（Veronique Benei）编，《东方在西方》（*East in West*），德里，Permanent Black 出版社，即将出版。

10 拉鲁·梅尔策（Lalou Meltzer），“过去的街道”（Past Street），见西拉杰·拉素尔（Ciraj Rasool）和桑德拉·普罗萨兰迪（Sandra Prosalendis）编：《回忆开普敦的社区》（*Recalling Community in Cape Town*），开普敦，第六区博物馆出版，2001 年，21-22 页。

11 琼安·斯考特的论文《经验的明证》看起来做出了这个假设。

公共文化与历史的未来

一直以来，流行文化研究都给历史学家带来方法论上的挑战，这些挑战有时会导致对学科协议的数量可观的重新思考。今天的流行文化更像卡洛尔·贝肯内吉（Carol Breckenridge）和阿君·阿帕杜莱（Arjun Appadurai）曾经称作“公共文化”的那种东西，如果通过这样一个表达我们指的是媒体与“文化”生产之间的密切关联——二者，正是过去一百年的标志性特征——的话。这里我要尝试作出的是一些关于公共文化和学院历史学科的未来之间的关系的思索。

到十九世纪中期，历史在西方成为一门专门学科的时候，它必然发展出与书面文字的密切联系。历史学家开始把一些书面的文本看作他们的“一手”（史料）来源。档案馆就是储藏这些文献的机构。通过给所有人对文献同等的使用机会而服务于善意的（bona fide）研究者的机构这一观念本身就意味着，从逻辑和历史上来说，档案馆将发展成为公共的、国有的机构。确实，在1919年贾杜纳斯·萨卡尔（Jadunath Sarkar）爵士与其他人一起着手建立印度历史记录委员会（Indian Historical Records Commission）——作为印度档案运动重要的一部分——的时候，他就经常强调收集政府和私人记录，对这些记录登记分类并为印度历史的研究而保存这些记录的档案馆的“公共”（因而为国有）性质。然而，自贾杜纳斯爵士的时代，尤其是自第二次世界大战以来，情况发生了很大的变化。民众对一个更民主、更加去殖民化的世界的要求的抬头，导致了对历史学家关于档案馆的观念的重要而隐蔽的修正。在这个学科在战争年代为使“普通”人民的日常生活成为其原则性的旨趣之一而扩大其范围的时候，它也不得不拓展“档案（馆）”的概念并试图发掘一些新的解读方式。因为甚至在具备书写传统的社会中，“普通人”的日常生活不会以类似于政治、军事或社会精英之生活的方式在档案中留下可追溯的痕迹，历史学家们被迫在他们的学科之外寻找证据。他们注意到了与物质文化、文化实践、口头和其他非书写形式的记忆相关的信息。谈到这种使非精英人物成为历史主题的开风气之先的著作，人们可能会想到G·H·D·柯尔（G. H. D. Cole）和雷蒙德·波斯特盖特（Raymond Postgate）的《常人》（*The Common People*，1938年）。就近的说，孟加拉历史学家尼哈兰詹·雷（Niharranjan Ray）的大作《bangalir itihash》［《孟加拉人民史》（*A History of the Bengali People*），这本书写于二十世纪四十年代，但直到最近才被约翰·胡德（John Hood）译成英文］可被认为在印度历史上具有与之类似的地位。柯尔和波斯特盖特集中于自十八世纪晚期以来“常人”生活的“政治和经济方面”而刻意地忽视了对“艺术，文学和科学”的一切探讨。换言之，他们并没有集中研究“流行文化”；他们寻找的经济和政治的信息可以很容易地从官方的档案中找到。另一方面，雷则使孟加拉人民的观念、艺术、文学以及物质文化成为其研究的核心主题。他的档案观也相应地更为宽广。他挖掘文本和碑铭的信息，也重视关于考古学、物理地理学以及古钱币的信息以对精英集团之外的孟加拉人在过去如何生活作出合理的猜测。当然，在深入那些并无可用的一手记录的过去时，把目光转向其他学科来提供关于这些过去曾在何处被归档（姑且这么说）的线索，是完全合理的。

甚至对于那些书写记录大量可用的时期——比如说西欧和其他地方的资本主义体制兴起时期——无论在城市还是乡村，流行文化的主题都对历史学家提出了挑战。重建不同社会中的现代化或“早期现代性”的体制史是一回事，但人们该去哪里发掘，比如说工人如何经历这种现代性——如果他们并没有给我们留下日记、文学或自传？历史学家凭借精彩的创造力对这些任务做出了回应，并因此而帮助更新了这个学科。尤金·韦伯（Eugene Weber），凯思·托马斯爵士（Keith Thomas），爱德华·汤普森（Edward Tompson），罗伯特·达恩顿（Robert Darnton），娜塔莉·泽蒙·戴维斯（Natalie Davis）朝向人类学的道路发展；戴维斯和卡洛·京茨堡（Davis and Carlo Ginzburg）则开发出微历史的研究领域（这个术语也可以用来描述年鉴学派的晚期作品）；格雷格·丹宁（Greg Dening），马歇尔·萨林斯（Marshall Sahlins），莱斯·艾萨克（Rhys Isaac），多纳·莫瑞克（Donna Merwick），英加·克兰迪宁（Inga Clendinen）及其他学者则走向了民族志的历史研究。扬·凡西纳（Jan Vansina），通过对非洲语境的研究，向我们展示了如何解读口头传统来重构过去。拉纳吉特·古哈（Ranajit Guha），在对十九世纪殖民地印度农民的“造反意识”的研究中为寻找可能解开造反实践之谜的工具而转向了结构主义和语义学。汤普森和霍布斯鲍姆以及他们那一辈的其他学者——以及后来的二十世纪七十年代的女性主义者——强调恢复被边缘化了的人民对社会变革的经验的重要性并自然地走向了对“口述史”研究的发展。保罗·汤普森（Paul Thompson）的著作《过去的声音》（*The Voice of the Past*，1978年）描绘了这场运动的精神。口述史被证明在检视城市工人阶级或农民以及部落和土著民族的过去方面非常有助益。

但甚至这些进步也在我们关于档案的思想方面产生了一些不可预见的后果。一度看来是放眼超越传统档案的聪明而简单的举动，在某些情形下却对人们对档案本身的观念提出了新的疑问。例如，“口述史”并不一定引出漂亮地填补档案之间的空白并同可用书面文献互补的信息。与其说记忆起到了补充作用，倒不如说它增补了书面文献。也就是说，与简单地填补书面文献的空白相反，记忆既在后者中补充那些缺失的东西，又同样地把人们的注意力引向这些文献的局限。到二十世纪八九十年代，人们日益认识到，记忆和历史不会列出一份整洁的印度档案。有的记忆是寻求来的，而有的记忆是被发现的。正如保罗·里克尔（Paul Ricoeur）在他最近关于这个主题的书中指出的那样；它既包括回忆又包含遗忘。此外，许多记忆也可能是不自觉的。在东南亚研究中，沙希德·阿明（Shahid Amin）关于乔里乔拉事件（Chauri Chaura）的研究，阿贾伊·斯卡里亚（Ajay Skaria）关于旦吉比尔人（Dangi Bhils），关于丽图·梅农（Ritu Menon）、乌尔瓦西·布塔利亚（Urvashi Butalia）、阿克姆拉·巴森（Akmla Bhasin）和贾南德达·潘帝（Gyanendra Pandey）关于印巴分治（Partition）及其记忆的研究——无疑人们还可以援引其他的例子——直接就口述史如何完全区别于历史学科这一问题作出了回应。这样就好像流行文化，以其对记忆和口口相传的强调，以诸种在根本上与官方档案程序的构成原则迥异的方式记录了人们的生活传统。尽管，正如沙希德·阿明在他的《事件、隐喻和记忆》（*Event, Metaphor, Memory*，1995 年）中富有教益地提醒我们注意的那样，人民的和官方的一直处于对话状态之中。

正如对电影和电视出现之前的大众文化的研究一度革新了历史家有关档案化过去的实践与体制的思考，今天我们也可能恰巧处在一个类似的、同历史学的未来息息相关的关键时刻。如果历史学家在一百年后出现并且想要撰写我们自己的、当代的流行文化史，会发生什么？现在的流行文化的信息库是什么？可能在当今世界的每一个部分，流行文化都近乎大众文化。它已经——或正在——受到电影、电视、视频和网络以及电子世界越来越多的设备的影响。这不是说全世界都是同样的情形。解释为什么世界各地的流行文化尽管受到媒体的全球性影响，却依然不尽相同；或者，全球化何以如此讽刺：有时有助于创造这种巨大的、全球性的差异的政治（在所谓的西方和伊斯兰之间，比如说，按照来自双方的一些极端主义者的说法），这确实将是历史学家的任务。但无论故事得到怎样的讲述，媒体在其中扮演的将是决定性的角色。

如果这是真的，那么可以推论，未来历史学家将更多地是一个媒体分析者而不是文字匠。未来研究二十世纪或更晚的时代的历史学家需要在理解以下几方面加以训练：媒体如何运作，视觉和声音效果（而不只是语词）如何生产政治论点并让大众信服。人们能否在不考虑媒体的情况下理解二战后的民族主义？如此多的当今全球政治，如果没有媒体的话都难以想象：南非真相与和解的政治，澳大利亚的对原住民说“对不起”的饱受争议的政治，日韩或日中之间调节各自战时记忆的政治，以及伊拉克的两次战争。体制上，我已经看到对此情况开始有学术回应。现在我们有撰写多媒体博士论文的学生（这让我们这一代学者措手不及，因为我们没有评估此类学位论文必需的技能）。现在我们有一茬更年轻的体育和文化史学家，他们最关注的是媒体在关联地方、国家和全球的过程中扮演的角色。在德里发展中社会研究中心的萨莱（Sarai）学者群以及那些与班加罗尔文化与社会研究中心有联系的学者[1]——仅举此两例——看起来正在这个方向上实验。在印度史研究领域，我们有拉维·瓦苏德万（Ravi Vasudevan）的例子，他实际上已经领先于他的时代——不辞辛劳地在电影和历史分析的方法上训练自己。简言之，我预计历史学家和媒体分析者之间的沟壑在未来将越来越小，而且这是出于必要。更遑论这样的事实了：未来的历史学家将比像我自己这样的人——对我们来说，电脑仍只是一种被推崇的打字机——更具备应用计算机知识。总之，未来的历史学家，将属于美国历史学家罗伯特·罗森斯通（Robert Rosenstone）所谓的后文字世界。后文字世界的人具备识字能力但并不读书，因为他们在媒体中长大并更喜欢通过媒体来表达他们自己。

这不是说“传统”历史学家是那些即将得知自己将会灭绝的那些人。相反，这里说的是，研究当代流行文化的历史学家将不得不同样严肃地涉入媒体研究，正如汤普森那一带的历史学家涉入文化人类学的研究那样。反过来，他们会有新问题有待处理。流行文化与数码研究的紧密关联将提出新的数据储存和调取问题，问题不仅在于电子世界产生的信息的高度扩散。讽刺的是，问题也在于此类数据瞬息即逝的性质。已开始研究电子档案的历史学家已经报告了因为技术飞速进步导致电子存储方式过时，或者因转换存储格式的成本过高而带来的信息严重损毁。电子储存方式很可能比在许多过去和现时社会中发现的口头传播方式更加转瞬即逝。波你尼（Panini，约公元前四世纪印度的梵文语法学家）或《吠陀经》(Vedas)可能不受歪曲地以口头的方式流传成百上千个世纪，但对电子传播来说则不一定如此。把媒体当作档案馆来使用的未来历史学家可能不得不与本身就相当新颖的体制和技术的遗忘形式作斗争。因此反过来记忆研究领域也可能必须发生彻底的改动。

这就是我作为一名历史学家所看到的，这里呈现的这些短篇论文的结集的重要性之所在。研究今天为媒体所塑造的流行文化的不同方面的学者正在为明天改观的历史学科打下基础。

(翻译：王立秋　　审校：陈恒)

注释：

1 萨莱（Sarai）是德里发展中社会研究中心2000年启动的一个项目。Sarai在中亚和南亚诸语言中是“驿站”的意思。——校注现在何在？

我想讨论在许多广泛流传的评论中都看得到的两种关注：把当下理解为对未来的指导——一种历史化的努力——的倾向以及对政治存在的关注（也就是说，努力解决批评的社会目标）。罗伯特·皮平（Robert Pippin）引用黑格尔的《法哲学》（*Philosophy of Right*）说："哲学就是它自己在思想中得到理解的时间"。批评与缜密的哲学不是一回事。但就我们所面临的情况而言，它确实受到了黑格尔的断言的精神影响。批评必须反映它自己的时代。它既要阐释世界也要对世界说话。这就是有效批判的条件。批判必须厘清现在。"活在我们的世纪并为我们的世纪劳作"，凯瑟琳·斯蒂姆森（Catharine Stimpson）是这么说的。我们的评注者共享一种对命名、指派即描述我们经历的时间 / 带或时期的能力的关注。

大多数评论假设某种特定的当下之定义。科学和技术对此定义来说是关键性的。汤姆·米切尔（Tom Mitchell）极富启发性的起始问题定下了基调："理论"在媒体、生物科技和资本主义本身的逻辑发生的"剧变"面前已经变成"精神理疗（therapeutic）"和怯懦了吗？无论理论是否已经变得怯懦，许多论者都同意米切尔对当下的理解。汉森指向为"循环以及随技术发展的到来而发生的技术创新史无前例的加速，以及它所具有的毁灭和奴役的力量"所创造的境况。杰罗姆·麦克甘（Jerome McGann）、伊丽莎白·亚伯（Elizabeth Abel）、罗琳·达斯顿（Lorraine Daston）、斯蒂姆森、J·希利斯·米勒（J. Hillis Miller）以及其他学者都主张人文学科应涉入这些科学和通讯技术的新发展，并超越这些领域而深入经济学、理性选择理论、灵长类动物学的领域。

划分时代（periodizing）的本能与政治的本能有着深层次的联系。“就其（思考）致力于厘清现在——也就是说，世界之谜——而言”，劳丽蒂斯（Lauretis）写道，“理论的思考也是政治的”。因此我们对我们当下进行断代与我们如何想象政治也是相互关联的。反之亦然：一切对政治的想象都隐含某种对当下的勾勒。这就是为何，在我们以特定的方式定义当下开始，作为我们分析的第一步的时候，我们在某种意义上就已经使我们自己对一些特定的政治理念作出了承诺。然而，这些政治理念本身，也许需要比人们假设的还要更多的拷问。

编委会成员的声明珍视一种磋商式民主的理念，其中，以大学为基地的人文学者们扮演了公共知识分子的角色，旨在于推进社会正义和民主的事业。哈里·哈鲁图尼恩（Harry Harootunian）因此对理论的社会政治用途进行了解释：“《批评探索》所能做的……是为恢复理论作为开展试图想象一种关于现代性的话语——这种话语将对学界外的世界说话——的艰苦劳动的条件的真正使命提供一个论坛”。甚至玛丽·普维（Mary Poovey）对一份更加严肃的、仅限学院圈子的《批评探索》的审慎呼吁——“为同人（和我们的学生）而写是合适的”——设想了一个超验（尽管是学术的）的公众，起到“对人性含义的集体理解”的典藏作用。

普维的规劝之意得到了很好的理解，但她的陈述却引发政治的问题，因为甚至学术的、对人性含义的“集体理解”都会被我们迥异而冲突的人类集体性之愿景所分裂。而这就是政治的角色所在，即使是在学术 - 公共知识分子在大众媒体中总是与作家保持距离的情况下。当然，七八十年代后结构主义、解构和后殖民主义的流行本身至少在某种程度上也归功于这样的预期，即这些理论只会使我们的民主想象更加彻底地民主。想象福柯给《反俄狄浦斯》写的那个颠覆性的前言!

然而，由于我本人既来自某个想象中的西方又来自这个西方之外——我觉得我们的陈述中有令人不安的地方：我们过于情愿假设当下和政治都很容易被预言出来。就好像《批评探索》所需要做的，不过是找到某种能够充分满足我们对当下和政治的预示所需要的实践形式而已。我是从两个相互矛盾的视角来解读哈鲁图尼恩对“理论的真正使命”的描述的。某种分裂影响到我对当下的感知。有点类似于皮平在他的陈述中描述的那种消极的条件，但它却有一种不同的纲领性含义。

分裂包含了这些内容。我在头脑里设想的一个现代社会的规范性的图景，典型地且必然地起源于欧洲或西方。我通过一种这样一种智识传统来思考：人们在其中能够——至少是在原则上——清楚地提出建立在先验基础上（举例：对马克思来说是哥达纲领，而对罗尔斯来说则是正义）的正义的社会秩序的宽泛构成。我用这个蓝图去批判现存的不平等。但我也承认，今天存在这样一些在世界各地塑造大众政治的想象，避开或超出了我们对政治的规范性理解。这些想象既不属于左派也不属于右派。但它们对世界的管制来说都具有全球性的含义。基地组织就是一例。阿希尔·姆邦贝（Achille Mbembé）已对制造对许多非洲后殖民国家的社会再生产来说处于核心地位的，现代形式的作战和杀戮的“死亡力量（necropower）”作出了评论。[1] 就近而言，对我来说，是印度所谓的贱民（或以前的不可触摸者）和“落后”种姓的政治。先前的被压迫者——而且从很多方面看，如今他们依然受压迫——印度的低级种姓，多亏了印度选举民主的功用，在许多地方都对传统的等级制度和权威构成了挑战，但却没有没有必然地生产出作为一名学院知识分子的我认为是好的或正义的治理形式。这些政治动员不是右翼的；它们也不属于任何正统意义上的左翼。我也可以从就此给出来自其他我还略知一二的政治场景的一些具有可比性的例子：当代澳大利亚原住民为承认与正义而作出的斗争。

关于这些在世界许多地方——而不仅仅是南半球——出现的新的政治构造，指出这点是很重要的，即它们与理论阶级的交互行动并不仅仅是后者对前者说话的问题。事实上，这些新的政治阵营不再为寻求政治生活中的指导而把目光投向大学里的理论阶级。他们使用我们的修辞、技能和服务，但仅仅是以纯粹实用的方式。它们有他们自己计算自己行动得失的方式。他们所做的一切有纪念化和训导的一面。但他们并不与任何理论版的全球性主体一致；他们不是无产阶级，也不是哈特和内格里说的“诸众”。他们的行动出于他们的正义感，但他们对什么是正义的理解却是断裂的、语境化的，而且总是变动着。

我并不是在老生常谈。在学术人士与“人民大众”之间一直存在一道鸿沟。这道鸿沟对民主理论的学生来说是根本性的。长期以来马克思主义者都就自发性与组织建构了关于这道鸿沟理论。它也是福柯和德勒兹在六八年五月中的对话的主题。然而，总体上看，即便在民主国家内部，权力结构也使得理论阶级丝毫没有失掉对其判断和仲裁能力的自信。他们一直能假设这样的立场，如哈鲁图尼恩所言，对大学外听众说话的立场，假设这些听众会对我们所要说的感兴趣，或者假设至少我们可以教给他们关涉政治的东西。人们假设，让人接触在对世界的状态的理性阐发，将有助于人们理性地行事。这一直以来都是左派的真理罗曼史。

弗朗西斯·弗格森（Frances Ferguson）指出我们可能“已经完全过了这样的一个时代——在这个时代里，更广泛地散布更多的信息将带来像我们……告诉自己的关于越南的故事那样的故事”。基地组织、印度的贱民和澳大利亚的原住民都乐于在方便的时候实用地利用学者，但他们并不在学界任何形式的训导之下。这把我们——理论阶级——置于一个特殊的情境之中。专业人士与人民大众之间不再可能进行任何只以我们的条件进行的政治对话。世界已经跨过了那个点。世界各地的人民已经通过不同的方式采用了权利和民主观念，并使之服务于我们可能永远也不会认为是（严格意义上说的）民主的事业；想想在阿富汗战争期间支持塔利班的“大规模示威”吧——一种我们同大众的意愿表达和以朝向民主的运动联系在一起的动员形式！这类事件大多在所谓西方的边界之外发生。这些发展对西方来说具有深远的意义，这点已为 2001 年 9 月 11 日的事件及自那时起发生的事件所佐证。

然而，这些发展本身却没有给予我们任何可以用来对它们进行评价的普世的、规范化的视野。在我们应要求对世界作出评判的时候，我们并没有学术上可信的东西来替代那些我们在大学中争论的原本属于西方的普世原则。在我看来，今天理论与实践之间的脱节并不仅仅是对现实未能符合我们的范畴这个古老问题的重现。因此，这也不是《批评探索》能否找到一种与其时代相符的政治的问题。当然，未来的理论与批评必须正视科技发展，特别是与传播技术变革。但正如“二十一世纪美国学者”并不仅仅是一个的美国地方性人物而同时也是一个包含世界的人，理论也将不得不同现今在政治领域超出“西方”政治思想的控制的那些东西竞争。因为只有通过承认今日政治的混浊不堪，我们才能让一个如此多元以至于不会为单一的定义所穷尽的当下成型。

带着这些想法，我建议《批评探索》可以对以下两个额外的领域进行积极的关注：

民主的全球和异质想象。南半球的政治理论家们已经用平民、雅各宾式的民主或者过度的政治化来描述对人们熟悉的民主形式的流行用途会导致的后果。负面的形容词——平民式的，过度的——指向这样一个事实：政治领域如今已不对应于任何政治的预设想法。这种不对称性（noncommensurability）需要更多的注意。

政治宗教。在9/11后我不需要对此进行过度的说明。塔拉尔·阿萨德（Talal Asad）新近关于世俗这一概念的著作和布鲁斯·林肯（Bruce Lincoln）的著作《神圣的恐怖》（Holy Terrors）都以各自的方式强调了信仰在引导当代政治想象中的重要性。《批评探索》中的理论需要穿越政治“神学”地带。[2]

(翻译：王立秋)

注释：

1 参见阿希尔·姆邦贝，后殖民论》（*On the Postcolony*），伯克利，2001 年。

2 参见塔拉尔·阿萨德，《世俗的形成：基督教，伊斯兰教，现代性》（*Formations of the Secular: Christianity, Islam, Modernity*），加州，斯坦福大学出版社，2003 年；以及布鲁斯·林肯，《神圣的恐怖：在 9/11 后思考宗教》（*Holy Terrors: Thinking about Religion after September 11*），芝加哥大学出版社，2003 年。

Belatedness as Possibility:

Subaltern Histories, Once Again

I

Even though I will be discussing historiography, not art, in the main body of this essay, I have to acknowledge that the essay owes its title to the accident of an invitation I received recently from the noted historian of visual culture in South Asia, Professor Christopher Pinney, to speak at a conference on art history he had organized at the Northwestern University in Chicago in May 2008. The topic of belatedness was being discussed at the conference, and the invitation made me remember that my most recent encounter with the theme of belatedness was at an exhibition of Indian art held in Chicago in 2007.

A marvelous exhibition of "contemporary art from India" was held at the Chicago Cultural Center that year. The art works of Gulammohammed Sheikh, Nalini Malani, Subodh Gupta, Vivan Sundaram and others were impressive and brilliant in their own right. But the catalogue of the exhibition, *New Narratives: Contemporary Art from India* made it clear what the sense of time was that underwrote words like "new" or "contemporary."[1] Indian art could be "contemporary" because, as the curator, Betty Seid, put it in her introduction to the volume, it "reflect[ed] her [India's] world recognition as a major player in the new millennium." American museums had avoided purchasing or exhibiting contemporary Indian art until it became truly contemporary, something that had moved from being "stuck in an ethnographic mode of self-comparison" to a state where "contemporary artists from India *of the world* happen to be living and working in India."[2] So "Western curators of contemporary art" are now "beginning to catch on about India" but it is easy to see why: they are catching on because Indian artists are, at long last, catching up!

Has the curse of belatedness been ever lifted from India, I wondered? The same catalogue goes on to speak of the history of modernism and feminist art in India thus: "Like Modernism, feminist art came to India later than to the West."[3] Indian art does not become "global" or of "the world" until it arrives at the point that is recognized in the West as "contemporary" — a point at which the West presumably has always been, at least long before Indian art got there. "The communication capabilities of our electronic age have provided global cognition of the art-making world that was unavailable to many mid-twentieth century artists of India," the catalogue essay explains, and continues:

Before independence in 1947, Western modern art was virtually unknown in India. Indian artists had not been exposed to the gradual evolution of modern art history. Rather, they were bombarded with the entirety of it, with exhibitions in India and with newly available opportunities to study and travel abroad.[4]

I felt honored by Professor Pinney's invitation but, for me, it spoke to the issue of belatedness in ways both formal and personal. I was, first of all, a belated choice for the conference. Their second keynote speaker absented himself at the last moment and I was parachuted into the conference to fill the gap. I felt I was in a situation somewhat similar to what the All India Radio once used to describe as being "in the place of the scheduled artiste." I was invited most cordially but belatedly — not anybody's fault; but that was how it worked out. Besides, some of the themes adumbrated in the conference-statement Professor Pinney had circulated also spoke to the idea of belatedness. The conference, the statement said, was meant to be window into "the logic of a certain sort of historiographic practice." Certain modes of art production get disqualified from the canons of art history by being seen as "belated" — modernism in India would be an example, I presumed. "Is there a single temporality at stake?" the statement asked. In fact, it was issued in a spirit of rebellion against any such judgment: "Is the putatively universalizing space of the white cube itself only a EuroAmerican fantasy ...? Would a global practice dictate a heterogeneity which eschewed the possibility of the 'global'? ... Can territories be abandoned in favor of 'flows'?" And it also met the question of judgment head on: "How can the attributions of value occur in unfamiliar aesthetic worlds? ... Are such attributions ... necessary to a World Art?"[5]

So in agreeing to speak belatedly about belatedness, I was reminded of a joke in my home-town of Calcutta. Bengali senior citizens are often addressed by adding a respectful "da" at the end of their names: thus Ashisda for Ashis Nandy, or Ranajitda for Ranajit Guha. When Derrida visited the city a few years ago to inaugurate and speak at a book fair, people ignorant of foreign ways assumed that he was probably an older Bengali man whose real name was "Deri," a word that in Bangla quite appropriately means "delay," and that it was as a mark of respect that he was called "Deri-da." So when it was clear that I could be at the conference only in somebody else's place, the chain of association to the noted philosopher led me to one of the thoughts that I will be elaborating in this essay — the relationship between belatedness and displacement, for I do think that it is through that connection that belatedness becomes an opportunity, or a "possibility," an association I gesture towards in the title of this essay.

The questions raised by Professor Pinney in his conference statement reverberate in the halls of subaltern histories that I frequent in the course of my work as a historian. The theme of belatedness and a certain spirit of rebellion against it were written all over *Subaltern Studies*. That discussion was a critical part of the process through which *Subaltern Studies*, a series that we could once think of only ever as an *Indian* project, became a part of global or world-history. So while Professor Pinney's conference bracketed the word "world" in the expression "(World) Art," let me speak of the world as it gets constituted when we convert belatedness into possibilities. You will see that the same problem of judgment that occurs in art history when the trope of belatedness is used occurs in political historiography as well: How do we evaluate developments in subaltern history as that history becomes part of an emergent global formation?

II

Right from the moment of its birth, *Subaltern Studies* was greeted by several commentators as a "belated" project, carrying out in the subcontinent what British "history from below" had accomplished a long time ago. Arif Dirlik was one of the better known of these critics. Belatedness in history was not a new problem as such. Alexander Gerschenkron, the reputed

Harvard historian who wrote a book in the early nineteen sixties, *Economic Backwardness in Historical Perspective*, saw the problem of Russian modernization through the prism of belatedness and the politics of having to "catch up" with the more "modern" nations.[6] The Indian Prime Minister Nehru would often say after independence that India had to accomplish in decades what the Americans had achieved over a few hundred years. "Belatedness," as I tried to argue in *Provincializing Europe*, was an integral part of a certain kind of historicist outlook that was born in the nineteenth century. As my quotations from the catalogue volume of last year's exhibition in Chicago will have shown, the outlook still informs discussions of art history in the public realm.

The problem of belatedness speaks to a problem of repetition and re-cognition in history. If something happens that resembles something else within a field that is conceptually structured by before-after relationships, then that which comes later is seen as belated. This in turn raises a question that Homi Bhabha once asked, using Rushdie's words with some sense of urgency: How does newness enter the world?[7] How do we know what is new in what seems like repetition?

I want to submit to you two propositions that may seem a little paradoxical. My first proposition is that newness enters the world through acts of displacement. My second proposition is that newness confounds judgment because judgment tends to see the new as repetition and therefore deficient. Newness is hard to distinguish from a simulacrum, a fake that is neither a copy nor original. To be open to the new is to engage in a Heideggerian struggle: to hear that which I do not already understand. Judgment, and in my case I mean political judgment, makes this a very difficult task. In the rest of this essay I will elaborate and explain my propositions by using *Subaltern Studies* as an example.

Before I do so, however, it may be helpful to take a page out of Gilles Deleuze, surely someone who has in our times thought more than most about some of these questions. Deleuze makes a primary distinction between "repetition" and "generality" in order to make a further distinction between "repetition" and "resemblance." "Repetition is not generality," he says and adds: "Repetition and resemblances are different in kind — extremely so." Generality, according to Deleuze, "presents two major orders: the qualitative order of resemblances and the quantitative order or equivalences. Cycles and equalities are their respective symbols." Repetition, on the other hand, refers to "non-exchangeable and non-substitutable singularities." To repeat "is to behave in a certain manner, but in relation to something unique or singular that has no equal or equivalent."[8]

> *If exchange is the criterion of generality, theft and gift are those of repetition. ... This is the apparent paradox of festivals: they repeat an 'unrepeatable'. They do not add a second or third time to the first, but carry the first time to the 'nth' power.... [I] t is not the Federation Day which commemorates or represents the fall of the Bastille, but the fall of the Bastille which celebrates and repeats in advance all the Federation Days; or Monet's first water lily which repeats all the others. Generality, as generality of the particular, thus stands opposed to repetition as universality of the singular. The repetition of a work of art is like singularity without a concept, and it is not by chance that a poem must be learned by heart.*[9]

The distinction hinted at in this passage between law and poetry, history and memory, is what gives repetition its power to transgress. "The theatre of repetition is opposed to the theatre of representation, just as movement is opposed to the concept and to representation which refers it back to the concept."[10] Deleuze makes it clear that repetition is how newness enters the world but it does so in disguise and through displacement — "disguise no less than displacement forms part of repetition"

— for repetition (this is Deleuze's reading of Kierkegaard and Nietzsche) is "the double condemnation of habit and memory" both of which, as we shall see, underlie political judgment.[11] Repetition thus constitutes a crisis of political judgment.

III

Now I want to elaborate the themes of displacement and disguise, the two aspects of Deleuzian repetition, through the example of *Subaltern Studies*. First, let me document the theme of displacement and then I will turn to the more difficult question of disguise.

Subaltern Studies, the series with which I have been associated since 1982, was an instance of politically motivated historiography. Political judgment was central to this project. It came out of a Marxist tradition of history-writing in South Asia and was markedly indebted to Mao and Gramsci in the initial formulations that guided the series. The tradition of history-writing on the Left in India was deeply, though perhaps unsurprisingly, influenced by English Marxist or socialist historiography, the so-called "history from below" tradition pioneered by the likes of Edward Thompson, Eric Hobsbawm, Christopher Hill, George Rudé, and others. Just as Thompson's work on English popular history was predicated on the question:

what contributions did the lower orders of society make to the history of English democracy?, so did historians in the *Subaltern Studies* series begin by asking a similar question: What contributions did the subaltern classes make on their own to the politics of nationalism in India, and hence to Indian democracy as well?[12] But here the similarity ended. English Marxist narratives of popular histories were moulded on a developmental idea of time: the peasant, in that story, either became extinct or was superseded to give rise to the worker who, through machine-breaking, Chartism, and other struggles for rights, one day metamorphosed into the figure of the citizen or the revolutionary proletariat. The peasant or tribal of the third-world who — as if through a process of telescoping of the centuries — suddenly had the colonial state and its modern bureaucratic and repressive apparatus thrust in his face, was, in this mode of thinking, a "pre-political" person. He or she was someone who did not, as it were, understand the operative languages of modern, governing institutions while having to deal with them. In terms of the English "history from below" propositions, it was only over time, and by undergoing a process of intellectual development, that the subaltern classes could mature into a modern political force.

Subaltern Studies began by repudiating this developmental

idea of "becoming political." The peasant or the subaltern, it was claimed, was *political* from the very instance they rose up in rebellion against the institutions of the Raj.[13] Their actions were political in the sense that they responded to and impacted on the institutional bases of colonial governance: the Raj, the moneylender, and the landlord. We did not then think much about the implications of our claim that the subaltern could be political without undergoing a process of "political development." Yet the implications of that claim were writ large on our historiography.

I should explain that the legacies of both imperialism and anti-colonialism speak to each other in this implicit debate about whether the subaltern became political over time (through some kind of pedagogic practice) or whether the figure of the subaltern was constitutionally political. Developmental time, or the sense of time underlying a stadial view of history, was indeed a legacy bequeathed by imperial rule in India. This is the time of the "not yet" as I called it *Provincializing Europe*. European political thinkers such as Mill (or even Marx) employed this temporal structure in the way they thought history. Nationalists and anti-colonialists, on the other hand, repudiated this imagination of time in the twentieth century in asking for self-rule to be granted right away, without a period of waiting or preparation, without delay, "now." What replaced the structure of the "not yet" in their imagination was the horizon of the "now."[14]

The British argued against giving self-rule to educated Indians in the nineteenth century by saying that they were not representative of the larger masses of the Indian "people".

The answer came from Gandhi who, following his entry into Indian politics during the First World War, made the main nationalist party, the Indian National Congress, into a "mass" organization. He did so by enlisting peasants as ordinary, the so-called "four-anna" members with voting rights within the party. The "mass base" of the Congress enabled its leaders to claim the status of being "representative" of the nation even if the poor and the non-literate formally did not have any electoral power under the Raj. The educational gap that separated the peasant from the educated leaders was never considered a problem in this idea of representation. The peasant, it was assumed, was fully capable of making citizenly choices that colonial rule withheld from him or her. From the very beginning of the 1920s, Gandhi spoke in favor of universal adult franchise in a future, independent India. The peasant would thus be made a citizen overnight (at least with respect to voting) without having to live out the developmental time of formal or informal education — that was the "now" the nationalists demanded.

In the constitutional debates that took place in the Constituent Assembly right after independence, the philosopher, and later statesman, Radhakrishnan argued for a republican form of government by claiming that thousand of years of civilisation had — even if formal education was absent — already prepared the peasant for such a state.[15]

What underwrote this anti-colonial but populist faith in the modern-political capacity of the masses was another European inheritance, a certain kind of poetics of history: romanticism. It is, of course, true that the middle-class leaders of anti-colonial movements involving peasants and workers never quite abandoned the idea of developmental time and a pedagogical project of educating the peasant. Gandhi's writings and those of other nationalist leaders often express a fear of the lawless mob and see education as a solution to the problem.[16] But this fear was qualified by its opposite, a political faith in the masses. In the 1920s and the 30s, this romanticism marked Indian nationalism generally — many nationalists who were not Communist or of the Left, for instance, would express this faith. Francesca Orsini, who works on Hindi literature, recently excavated a body of evidence documenting this tendency. To take but stray examples from her selection, here is Ganesh Shankar Vidyarthi (1890-1931), the editor of the Hindi paper

Pratap, editorializing on 31 May 1915:

The much-despised peasants are our true bread-givers [annadata], not those who consider themselves special and look down upon the people who must live in toil and poverty as lowly beings.[17]

Or Vidyarthi again on 11 January 1915:

Now the time has come for our political ideology and our movement not [to] be restricted to the English-educated and to spread among the common people [samanya janta], and for Indian public opinion [lokmat] to be not the opinion of those few educated individuals but to mirror the thoughts of all the classes of the country.... democratic rule is actually the rule of public opinion.[18]

One should note that this romantic-political faith in the masses was populist as well in a classical sense of the term. Like Russian populism of the late nineteenth century, this mode of thought not only sought a "good" political quality in the peasant, but also, by that step, worked to convert the so-called "backwardness" of the peasant into an historical advantage. The peasant, "uncorrupted" by the self-tending individualism of the bourgeois and oriented to the needs of his or her community, was imagined as already endowed with the capacity to usher in a modernity different and more communitarian than what was prevalent in the West.[19] The contradiction entailed in the very restricted nature of franchise under colonial rule and the simultaneous induction of the peasant and the urban poor into the nationalist movement had one important consequence. The very restrictions put on constitutional politics then meant that the field, the factory, the bazaar, the fair, and the street became major arenas for the struggle for independence and self-rule. And it is in these arenas that subaltern subjects with their characteristic modes of collective mobilization (that included practices of public violence) entered public life.

The inauguration of the age of mass-politics in India was thus enabled by ideologies that displayed some of the key global characteristics of populist thought. There was, firstly, the tendency to see a certain political goodness in the peasant or in the masses. And there was, in addition, the tendency also to see historical advantage where, by colonial judgment, there was only backwardness and disadvantage. To see "advantage" in "backwardness" — that is, to see belatedness as an opportunity — was also to challenge the time that was assumed by stadial views about history, it was to twist the time of the colonial "not yet" into the structure of the democratic and anti-colonial "now".

I give this potted history of the romantic-populist origins of Indian democratic thought — though not of Indian democracy as such and the distinction is important — to suggest a point fundamental to my exposition. The insistence, in the early volumes of *Subaltern Studies* (first published in 1982) and in Ranajit Guha's *Elementary Aspects of Peasant Insurgency in Colonial India* (1983), that the peasant or the subaltern was always-already political — and not "pre-political" in any developmentalist sense — was in some ways a recapitulation of a populist premise that was implicit in any case in the anti-colonial mass movements in British India.[20] But there was, in my sense, a displacement as well, of this term. The populism in *Subaltern Studies* was more intense and explicit. There was, first of all, no "fear of the masses" in *Subaltern Studies* analysis. Absent also — and this went against the grain of classically Marxist or Leninist analysis — was any discussion of the need for organization or a party. Guha and his colleagues drew inspiration from Mao (particularly his 1927 report on the peasant movement in the Hunan district) and Gramsci (mainly his *Prison Notebooks*). But their use of Mao and Gramsci speaks of the times when *Subaltern Studies* was born. This was, after all, the seventies: a period of global Maoism that Althusser and others had made respectable. Excerpts from Gramsci's notebooks had come out in English in 1971. Both Gramsci and Mao were celebrated as a way out of Stalinist or Soviet Marxism after Czechoslovakia of 1968. Many of the historians in *Subaltern Studies* were participants in or sympathizers of the Maoist movement that shook parts of India between 1969 and 1971.[21]

Yet, significantly, neither Mao's references to the need for "leadership of the Party" nor Gramsci's strictures against "spontaneity" featured with any degree of prominence in what we wrote. Guha's focus in his *Elementary Aspects of Peasant Insurgency* remained firmly on understanding how rebellious peasants mobilized themselves in ninenteenth-century British India, that is to say, before the age of Gandhian "mass nationalism". Guha sought to comprehend the peasant as a collective author of these uprisings by doing a structuralist analysis of the space — and time-creating practices of mobilization, communication, and public violence that constituted rebellion (and thus, for Guha, a subaltern domain of politics). There were limitations, from Guha's socialist point of view, to what the peasants could achieve on their own but these limitations did not call for the mediation of a party. A cult of rebellion marked the early efforts of *Subaltern Studies*, reminiscent of one of Mao's sayings that were popular during the Cultural Revolution: "to rebel is justified." Rebellion was not a technique for achieving something; it was its own end. Indeed, from a global perspective, one might say that *Subaltern Studies* was the last — or the latest — instance of a long global history of the Left: the romantic-popular search for a non-industrial revolutionary subject that was initiated in Russia, among other places, in the nineteenth century. This romantic populism shaped much of Maoism in the twentieth century, and left its imprint on the antinomies and ambiguities of Antonio Gramsci's thoughts on the Party as the Modern Prince.

The once-global and inherently romantic search for a revolutionary subject outside of the industrialized West has thus had a long history, traveling from Russia in the late nineteenth century to the colonial and semi-colonial (to use a Maoist expression) "third" world in the twentieth. The political potential of this romanticism is exhausted today. But looking back one can see what plagued this history of a search for a revolutionary subject in the relatively non-industrialized countries of the world. Such a subject by definition could not be the proletariat. Yet it was difficult to define a world-historical subject that would take the place of the industrial working classes that did not exist, not in great numbers anyway, in the peasant-based economies drawn into the gravitational pull of the capitalist world. Would the revolution, as Trotsky said, be an act of substitutionism? Would the Party stand in for the working classes? Could the peasantry, under the guidance of the party, be the revolutionary class? Would it be the category "subaltern" or Fanon's "the wretched of the earth"?

When the young, left-Hegelian Marx thought up the category of the proletariat as the new revolutionary subject of history that would replace the bourgeoisie — and he did this before Engels wrote his book on the Manchester working class in 1844 — there was a philosophical precision to the category. It also seemed to find a sociological correlate in working classes born of the industrial revolution. But names like "peasants" (Mao), "subaltern" (Gramsci) "the wretched of the earth" (Fanon), "the party as the subject" (Lenin/Lukacs) have neither philosophical nor sociological precision. It was as if the search for a revolutionary subject that was *not-the-proletariat* (in the absence of a large working class) was an exercise in a series of displacements of the original term, the proletariat. A telling case in point is Fanon himself. The expression "the wretched of the earth", as Fanon's biographer David Macey has pointed out, alluded to words of the Communist Internationale, in the song — " 'Debout, les damnés de la terrre'/ 'Arise, ye wretched of the earth' " — where it clearly referred to the proletariat. Yet Fanon used it to mean something else, something other than the proletariat. This other subject he could not quite define but he was clear that in the colony it could not be the proletariat. One only has to recall how, quite early on in his book, he cautioned: "Marxist analysis should always be slightly stretched every time we have to deal with the colonial problem."[22]

A collective subject with no proper name, a subject who can be named only through a series of displacements of the original European term "the proletariat" — this is a condition both of failure and of a new beginning. The failure is easy to see. It lies in the lack of specificity or definition. Where is the beginning? First of all, the very imprecision is a pointer to the inadequacy of Eurocentric thought in the context of a global striving for a socialist transformation of the world. Outside of the industrialized countries, the revolutionary subject was even theoretically undefined. The history of this imprecision amounts to the acknowledgment that if we want to understand the nature of popular political practices globally with names of subjects invented in Europe, we can only resort to a series of stand-ins (never mind the fact that original may have been a simulacrum as well). Why? Because we are working at and on the limits of European political thought even as we admit an affiliation to nineteenth-century European revolutionary romanticism. Recognizing the stand-in nature of categories like "the masses", " the subaltern" or "the peasant" is, I suggest, the first step towards writing histories of democracies that have emerged through the mass-politics of anticolonial nationalism. There is a mass-subject here, no doubt. But it can only be apprehended by consciously working through the limits of European thought. A straightforward search for a revolutionary world-historical subject only leads to stand-ins. The global and theoretical failure to find a proper name for the revolutionary subject that is not-the-proletariat thus inaugurates the need for new thought and research outside the West, resulting in a series of displacements of the once-European category, the proletariat.

IV

To sum up, then, much socialist political thought has been made possible outside of the West by a continual process of working through European categories in order to displace them from the locus of their original signification. So much for the theme of displacement that, as Deleuze reminded us, was a critical part of the transgressive power of repetition. But what about the theme of disguise?

The theme of disguise pertains to our capacity to name

and recognize the new. It is here that the tension (to speak with Deleuze) between generality and repetition, between law and poetry, between history/sociology and memory, reveals itself at its most intense and demonstrates how political judgment seeks to tame the new.

Consider once again the foundational text of *Subaltern Studies*, Ranajit Guha's *Elementary Aspects of Peasant Insurgency in Colonial India*. What is the status of the category "political" in Guha's (and our) polemic with Hobsbawm that the peasants and the tribals were not "pre-political," that they were in fact as political as the British or the middle classes?[23] The status is ambiguous: the peasants were political in the already-understood sense of the terms — in that they dealt with the institutions of colonial rule — but they were also "political" in some other sense about which we were not clear at all. The political claim that nineteenth-century peasant rebellions were political could only be made on the assumption — and this remains an assumption — that we already knew completely what 'being political' meant. What was new about peasant resistance in nineteenth-century India could only be expressed in the guise of the old category: "politics."

Something very similar happens — to cite a distant example that will show that the problem is more than historiographical or merely Indian — in the Australian historian Henry Reynold's path-breaking work on Aboriginal resistance to White occupation in nineteenth-century Australia. Take his book, *Fate of a Free People*, analyzing Aboriginal resistance in nineteenth-century Tasmania. Reynolds is aware of the European roots of the modern idea of the political. He writes how some European settlers were astonished to find among Aboriginals "ideas of their natural rights" which Reynolds regards, rightly, as European attempts at interpreting "in European terms" the world-making they encountered among the Aboriginals. Yet, in resisting histories written by earlier White historians and chroniclers, Reynolds, much like Guha, insists on the applicability of the category "political" in describing Aboriginal resistance. He challenges "the clear assumption that the Tasmanians were incapable of taking political action" and deliberately describes the nineteenth-century Aboriginal leader, Walter Arthur, as "the first Aboriginal nationalist," tearing the idea of "nationalism" from all its anchorage in the history of modern institutions.[24] Clearly, "politics" and "nationalism" are under-determined, part-sociological and part-rhetorical categories here, not completely open to the demand for clarification. And it is in their rhetorical imprecision that the disguising of the new happens.

Or take Partha Chatterjee's category of "the governed" —

again, a term in the series of displacements of the revolutionary subject that I have already traced before. Having documented the struggle for survival (including the stealing of electricity) — within which lessons are indeed learned by subaltern and other groups — that goes on everyday in the city of Calcutta, he suddenly, towards the end of his lectures on the theme, makes "the governed" the creators of something that even Aristotle might recognize: democracy. "What I have tried to show," he writes, "is that alongside the abstract promise of popular sovereignty, people in most of the world are devising new ways in which they can choose how they should be governed." He recognizes that "many of the forms of the political society" and their unlawful activities that he describes perhaps would not have met with "Aristotle's approval." Yet he believes that the "wise Greek," if he could see Chatterjee's evidence, might actually recognize an "ethical justification" for democracy in popular action that he might otherwise have disapproved of.[25] My point is, again, the ambiguity of this move, the claim that while popular action in everyday Calcutta does not always look democratic, it still heralds a democracy to come. It is, of course, entirely possible that everyday life in Calcutta looks forward to a future for which we just do not have a category yet. But in Chatterjee's prose, it is, once again, in the ambiguity of old and new uses of the word "democracy" that the actual "newness" of what goes on in Calcutta both shows and hides itself. Now we see it, now we don't.

My last example of disguise of the new is Hardt and Negri's well-known category of the "multitude," once again a candidate for inclusion in my list of terms that displace the original revolutionary subject of Europe. The disguise is ironical for a book that, in its first half, struggles — in a Deleuzian vein — to capture that which is about domination in the world: Empire. Yet their revolutionary agency "the multitude," while conceived of as immanent in a Spinozist way, has to acquire an "adequate consciousness" (resonances of Hegel-Marx here) in order to be political. "How can the actions of the multitude become political?" they ask. Their answer: "The only response we can give ... is that the action of the multitude becomes primarily political when it begins to confront directly and with *an adequate consciousness* the central repressive operations of Empire."[26]

I am then left to ask my final question: why does displacement combine with disguise to create the very structure of repetition? It goes back, I think, to a problem that Marx referred to a long time ago. Newness enters the world as a challenge to judgment and law. That is why Deleuze refers to it through the figure of poetry. Political judgment is tied to the old. It is salutary to remember that even Homi Bhabha, whose generative mediations on the postcolonial condition would not have much to say about the conditions for the struggle for socialism (as conventionally understood), began his journey as a postcolonial theorist with a gesture towards connecting with socialist politics as it was known in Britain in the 1980s.[27] I think Marx, in a moment of reflection on the problem of repetition and resemblance in history — and thus on the figure of the belated — put his finger on the necessary disguise of the new. The lines are very well known indeed but may bear repetition in the context of this discussion. Let me give Marx the final word with one minor qualification:

Men make their own history, but they do not make it just as they please.... The tradition of all the dead generations weighs like a nightmare on the brain of the living. And just when they seem ... engaged in creating something that has never yet existed, ... they anxiously conjure up the spirits of the past to their service and borrow from them names, battle cries and costumes in order to present the new scene of world history in this time-honoured disguise and this borrowed language.

Marx expects this process to have a happy Hegelian ending. He, as you know, compares this process to a person's experience of learning a new language: "a beginner who has learnt a new language always translates it back into his mother tongue, but he has assimilated the spirit of the new language and can freely express himself in it only when he finds his way in it without recalling the old and forgets his native tongue in the use of the new."[28] We are rightly suspicious of such happy endings. We remain interested in remainders and failures of translation that always come back to haunt and trouble what translation achieves. This is indeed where we may have to part with Marx and his progenies in contemplating the problem of repetition and belatedness in our time.

Thanks are due to the editors of this volume for their editorial suggestions.

Endnotes:

1. Betty Seid, *New Narratives: Contemporary Art from India* (Ahmedabad and Ocean Township, N.J.: Mapin, Grantha, 2007).

2. *New Narratives*, p.13

3. *New Narratives*, p. 15

4. *New Narratives*, p. 19.

5. Conference statement, "(World) Art: Art History and Global Practice," Northwestern University, 23-24 May 2008.

6. Alexander Gerschenkron, *Economic Backwardness in Historical Perspective — A Book of Essays* (Camb., Mass: Bellknap Harvard, 1962).

7. Homi Bhabha, "How Does Newness Enter the World?" in his *The Location of Culture*.

8. Gilles Deleuze, *Difference and Repetition*, trans. Paul Patton (New York: Columbia University Press, 1994), p.1.

9. Deleuze, *Difference*, pp.1-2.

10. Deleuze, *Difference*, p.10.

11. Deleuze, *Difference*, pp. xvi, 7.

12. See E.P. Thompson, *Whigs and Hunters*.

13. I discuss this in some detail in my essay "A Small History of *Subaltern Studies*" in my *Habitations of Modernity: Essays in the Wake of Subaltern Studies* (Chicago: The University of Chicago Press, 2002), Ch. 1.

14. See the discussion in the Introduction to my book *Provincializing Europe: Postcolonial Thought and Historical Difference* (Princeton, New Jersey: Princeton University Press,

2000).

15. See *Provinicializing Europe*, "Introduction" for details.

16. See Gyanendra Pandey's essay on the topic in Ranajit Guha and Gayatri Chakravorty Spivak eds, *Selected Subaltern Studies* (New York: Oxford University Press, 1988).

17. Francesca Orsini, "The Hindi Public Sphere and Political Discourse in the Twentieth Century", unpublished paper presented at a conference on "The Sites of the Political in South Asia", Berlin, October 2003

18. Ibid.

19. For an excellent discussion of this point, see Andrzej Walicki, *The Controversy Over Capitalism: Studies in the Social Philosophy of the Russian Populists* (Notre Dame, Indiana: University of Notre Dame Press, 1989), Chapters 1 and 2, in particular the section of "The Privilege of Backwardness."

20. Ranajit Guha, *Elementary Aspects of Peasant Insurgency in Colonial India* (Delhi: Oxford University Press, 1983), Chapter 1.

21. Shahid Amin, "De-Ghettoising the Histories of the non-West"; Gyan Prakash, "The Location of Scholarship"; in my "Globalization, Democracy, and the Evacuation of History?" in Jackie Assayag and Veronique Benei eds., *At Home in Diaspora: South Asian Scholars and the West* (Bloomington, Indiana: Indiana University Press, 2003).

22. Frantz Fanon, *The Wretched of the Earth*, trans., Constance Farrington (New York: Grove Press, 1963), p. 40.

23. Ranajit Guha, *Elementary Aspects of Peasant Insurgency in Colonial India* (Delhi: OUP, 1983), Chapter 1.

24. Henry Reynolds, *Fate of a Free People* (Ringwood, Victoria: Penguin, 1995), pp. 11, 23, 69.

25. Partha Chatterjee, *The Politics of the Governed: Reflections on Popular Politics in Most of the World* (New York: Columbia University Press, 2004), pp. 77-78.

26. Michael Hardt and Antonio Negri, *Empire* (Cambridge, Mass.: Harvard University Press, 2000), p.399.

27. Bhabha, "The Commitment to Theory".

28. Karl Marx, "The Eighteenth Brumaire of Louis Bonaparte," in Karl Marx and Frederick Engels, *Selected Works*, vol. 1 (Moscow: Progress Publishers, 1969), p. 398.

Postcoloniality and the Artifice of History: Who Speaks for "Indian" Pasts?

Push thought to extremes.

Louis Althusser

I

IT has recently been said in praise of the postcolonial project of *Subaltern Studies* that it demonstrates, "perhaps for the first time since colonization," that "Indians are showing sustained signs of reappropriating the capacity to represent themselves [within the discipline of history]."[1] As a historian who is a member of the *Subaltern Studies* collective, I find the congratulation contained in this remark gratifying but premature. The purpose of this article is to problematize the idea of "Indians" "representing themselves in history." Let us put aside for the moment the messy problems of identity inherent in a transnational enterprise such as *Subaltern Studies*, where passports and commitments blur the distinctions of ethnicity in a manner that some would regard as characteristically postmodern. I have a more perverse proposition to argue. It is that insofar as the academic discourse of history — that is, "history" as a discourse produced at the institutional site of the university — is concerned, "Europe" remains the sovereign, theoretical subject of all histories, including the ones we call "Indian," "Chinese," "Kenyan," and so on. There is a peculiar way in which all these other histories tend to become variations on a master narrative that could be called "the history of Europe." In this sense, "Indian" history itself is in a position of subalternity; one can only articulate subaltern subject positions in the name of this history.

While the rest of this article will elaborate on this proposition, let me enter a few qualifications. "Europe" and "India" are treated here as hyperreal terms in that they refer to certain figures of imagination whose geographical referents remain somewhat indeterminate.[2] As figures of the imaginary they are, of course, subject to contestation, but for the moment I shall treat them as though they were given, reified categories, opposites paired in a structure of domination and subordination. I realize that in treating them thus I leave myself open to the charge of nativism, nationalism, or worse, the sin of sins, nostalgia. Liberal-minded scholars would immediately protest that any idea of a homogeneous, uncontested "Europe" dissolves under analysis. True, but just as the phenomenon of orientalism does not disappear simply because some of us have now attained a critical awareness of it, similarly a certain version of "Europe," reified and celebrated in the phenomenal world of everyday relationships of power as the scene of the birth of the modern, continues to dominate the discourse of history. Analysis does not make it go away.

That Europe works as a silent referent in historical knowledge itself becomes obvious in a highly ordinary way. There are at least two everyday symptoms of the subalternity of non-Western, third-world histories. Third-world historians feel a need to refer to works in European history; historians of Europe do not feel any need to reciprocate. Whether it is an Edward Thompson, a Le Roy Ladurie, a George Duby, a Carlo Ginzberg, a Lawrence Stone, a Robert Darnton, or a Natalie Davis — to take but a few names at random from our contemporary world — the "greats" and the models of the historian's enterprise are always at least culturally "European." "They" produce their work in relative ignorance of non-Western histories, and this does not seem to affect the quality of their work. This is a gesture, however, that "we" cannot return. We cannot even afford an equality or symmetry of ignorance at this level without taking the risk of appearing "oldfashioned" or "outdated."

The problem, I may add in parenthesis, is not particular to historians. An unselfconscious but nevertheless blatant example of this "inequality of ignorance" in literary studies, for example, is the following sentence on Salman Rushdie from a recent text on postmodernism: "Though Saleem Sinai [of *Midnight's Children*] narrates in English... his intertexts for both writing history and writing fiction are doubled: they are, on the one hand, from Indian legends, films, and literature and, on the other, from the West — *The Tin Drum, Tristram Shandy, One Hundred Years of Solitude,* and so on."[3] It is interesting to note how this sentence teases out only those references that are from "the West." The author is under no obligation here to be able to name with any authority and specificity the "Indian" allusions that make Rushdie's intertexuality "doubled." This ignorance, shared and unstated, is part of the assumed compact that makes it "easy" to include Rushdie in English department offerings on postcolonialism.

This problem of asymmetric ignorance is not simply a matter of "cultural cringe" (to let my Australian self speak) on our part or of cultural arrogance on the part of the European historian. These problems exist but can be relatively easily addressed. Nor do I mean to take anything away from the achievements of the historians I mentioned. Our footnotes bear rich testimony to the insights we have derived from their knowledge and creativity. The dominance of "Europe" as the subject of all histories is a part of a much more profound theoretical condition under which historical knowledge is produced in the third world. This condition ordinarily expresses itself in a paradoxical manner. It is this paradox that I shall describe as the second everyday symptom of our subalternity, and it refers to the very nature of social science pronouncements themselves.

For generations now, philosophers and thinkers shaping the nature of social science have produced theories embracing the entirety of humanity. As we well know, these statements have been produced in relative, and sometimes absolute, ignorance of the majority of humankind — i.e., those living in non-Western cultures. This in itself is not paradoxical, for the more self-conscious of European philosophers have always sought theoretically to justify this stance. The everyday paradox of third-world social science is that *we* find these theories, in spite of their inherent ignorance of "us," eminently useful in understanding our societies. What allowed the modern European sages to develop such clairvoyance with regard to societies of which they were empirically ignorant? Why cannot we, once again, return the gaze?

There is an answer to this question in the writings of philosophers who have read into European history an entelechy of universal reason, if we regard such philosophy as the self-consciousness of social science. Only "Europe," the argument would appear to be, is *theoretically* (i.e., at the level of the fundamental categories that shape historical thinking) knowable; all other histories are matters of empirical research that fleshes out a theoretical skeleton which is substantially "Europe." There is one version of this argument in Edmund Husserl's Vienna lecture of 1935, where he proposed that the fundamental difference between "oriental philosophies" (more specifically, Indian and Chinese) and "Greek-European science" (or as he added, "universally speaking: philosophy") was the capacity of the latter to produce "absolute theoretical insights," that is "*theoria*" (universal science), while the former retained a "practical-universal," and hence "mythical-religious," character. This "practical-universal" philosophy was directed to the world in a "naive" and "straightforward" manner, while the world presented itself as a "thematic" to *theoria*, making possible a praxis "whose aim is to elevate mankind through universal scientific reason."[4]

A rather similar epistemological proposition underlies Marx's use of categories like "bourgeois" and "prebourgeois" or "capital" and "precapital." The prefix pre here signifies a relationship that is both chronological and theoretical. The coming of the bourgeois or capitalist society, Marx argues in the *Grundrisse* and elsewhere, gives rise for the first time to a history that can be apprehended through a philosophical and universal category, "capital." History becomes, for the first time, theoretically knowable. All past histories are now to be known (*theoretically*, that is) from the vantage point of this category, that is in terms of their differences from it. Things reveal their categorical essence only when they reach their fullest development, or as Marx put it in that famous aphorism of the *Grundrisse* :"Human anatomy contains the key to the anatomy of the ape."[5] The category "capital," as I have discussed elsewhere, contains within itself the legal subject of Enlightenment thought.[6] Not surprisingly, Marx said in that very Hegelian first chapter of Capital, vol. 1, that the secret of "capital," the category, "cannot be deciphered until the notion of human equality has acquired the fixity of a popular prejudice."[7] To continue with Marx's words:

Even the most abstract categories, despite their validity — precisely because of their abstractness — for all epochs, are nevertheless...themselves...a product of historical relations. Bourgeois society is the most developed and the most complex historic organization of production. The categories which express its relations, the comprehension of its structure, thereby also allow insights into the structure and the relations of production of all the vanished social formations out of whose ruins and elements it built itself up, whose partly still unconquered remnants are carried along within it, whose mere nuances have developed explicit significance within it, etc.... The intimations of higher development among the subordinate animal species... can be understood only after the higher development is already known. The bourgeois economy thus supplies the key to the ancient.[8]

For "capital" or "bourgeois," I submit, read "Europe."

II

Neither Marx nor Husserl spoke-not at least in the words quoted above — in a historicist spirit. In parenthesis, we should also recall here that Marx's vision of emancipation entailed a journey beyond the rule of capital, in fact beyond the notion of juridical equality that liberalism holds so sacred. The maxim "From each according to his ability to each according to his need" runs quite contrary to the principle of "Equal pay for equal work," and this is why Marx remains — the Berlin Wall notwithstanding (or not standing!) — a relevant and fundamental critic of both capitalism and liberalism and thus central to any postcolonial, postmodern project of writing history. Yet Marx's methodological/epistemological statements have not always successfully resisted historicist readings. There has always remained enough ambiguity in these statements to make possible the emergence of "Marxist" historical narratives. These narratives turn around the theme of "historical transition." Most modern third-world histories are written within problematics posed by this transition narrative, of which the overriding (if often implicit) themes are those of development, modernization, capitalism.

This tendency can be located in our own work in the *Subaltern Studies* project. My book on working-class history struggles with the problem.[9] Sumit Sarkar's (another colleague in the *Subaltern Studies* project) *Modern India*, justifiably regarded as one of the best textbooks on Indian history written primarily for Indian universities, opens with the following sentences:

The sixty years or so that lie between the foundation of the Indian National Congress in 1885 and the achievement of independence in August 1947 witnessed perhaps the greatest transition in our country's long history. A transition, however, which in many ways remains grievously incomplete, and it is with this central ambiguity that it seems most convenient to begin our survey.[10]

What kind of a transition was it that remained "grievously

incomplete"? Sarkar hints at the possibility of there having been several by naming three:

So many of the aspirations aroused in the course of the national struggle remained unfulfilled — the Gandhian dream of the peasant coming into his own in ***Ram-rajya*** *[the rule of the legendary and the ideal god-king Ram], as much as the left ideals of social revolution. And as the history of independent India and Pakistan (and Bangladesh) was repeatedly to reveal, even the problems of a complete bourgeois transformation and successful capitalist development were not fully solved by the transfer of power of 1947. (4)*

Neither the peasant's dream of a mythical and just kingdom, nor the Left's ideal of a social[ist] revolution, nor a "complete bourgeois transformation" — It is within these three absences, these "grievously incomplete" scenarios that Sarkar locates the story of modern India.

It is also with a similar reference to "absences" — the "failure" of a history to keep an appointment with its destiny (once again an instance of the "lazy native," shall we say?) — that we announced our project of Subaltern Studies:

It is the study of this ***historic failure of the nation to come***

***to its own**, a failure due to the **inadequacy** [emphasis added] of the bourgeoisie as well as of the working class to lead it into a decisive victory over colonialism and a bourgeois-democratic revolution of the classic nineteenth-century type . . . or [of the] "new democracy" [type] — **it is the study of this failure which constitutes the central problematic of the historiography of colonial India**.*[11]

The tendency to read Indian history in terms of a lack, an absence, or an incompleteness that translates into "inadequacy" is obvious in these excerpts. As a trope, however, it is an ancient one, going back to the hoary beginnings of colonial rule in India. The British conquered and represented the diversity of "Indian" pasts through a homogenizing narrative of transition from a "medieval" period to "modernity." The terms have changed with time. The "medieval" was once called "despotic" and the "modern," "the rule of law." "Feudal/capitalist" has been a later variant.

When it was first formulated in colonial histories of India, this transition narrative was an unashamed celebration of the imperialist's capacity for violence and conquest. To give only one example among the many available, Alexander Dow's *History of Hindostan*, first published in three volumes between

1770 and 1772, was dedicated to the king with a candor characteristic of the eighteenth century when one did not need a Michel Foucault to uncover the connection between violence and knowledge: "The success of Your Majesty's arms," said Dow, "has laid open the East to the researches of the curious."[12] Underscoring the connection between violence and modernity, Dow added:

The British nation have become the conquerors of Bengal and they ought to extend some part of their fundamental jurisprudence to secure their conquest... The sword is our tenure. It is an absolute conquest, and it is so considered by the world. (1:cxxxviii)

This "fundamental jurisprudence" was the "rule of law" that contrasted, in Dow's narrative, with a past rule that was "arbitrary" and "despotic." In a further gloss Dow explained that "despotism" did not refer to a "government of mere caprice and whim," for he knew enough history to know that that was not true of India. Despotism was the opposite of English constitutional government; it was a system where "the legislative, the judicial and the executive power [were] vested in the prince." This was the past of unfreedom. With the establishment of British power, the Indian was to be made a legal subject, ruled by a government open to the pressures of private property ("the foundation of public prosperity," said Dow) and public opinion, and supervised by a judiciary where "the distributors of justice ought to be independent of everything but law [as] otherwise the officer [the judge] becomes a tool of oppression in the hands of despotism" (l:xcv, cl, cxl-cxli).

In the nineteenth and twentieth centuries, generations of elite Indian nationalists found their subject positions, as nationalists, within this transition narrative that, at various times and depending on one's ideology, hung the tapestry of "Indian history" between the two poles of the homologous sets of oppositions, despotic/constitutional, medieval/modern, feudal/capitalist. Within this narrative shared between imperialist and nationalist imaginations, the "Indian" was always a figure of lack. There was always, in other words, room in this story for characters that embodied, on behalf of the native, the theme of "inadequacy" or "failure." Dow's recommendation of a "rule of law" for Bengal/India came with the paradoxical assurance (to the British) that there was no danger of such a rule "infusing" in the natives "a spirit of freedom":

To make the natives of the fertile soil of Bengal free, is beyond the power of political arrangement... Their religion, their institutions, their manners, the very disposition of their minds, form them for passive obedience. To give them property would only bind them with stronger ties to our interests, and make them our subjects; or if the British nation prefers the name-more our slaves. (1:cxl-cxli)

We do not need to be reminded that this would remain the cornerstone of imperial ideology for many years to come-subjecthood but not citizenship, as the native was never adequate to the latter-and would eventually become a strand of liberal theory itself.[13] This was of course where nationalists differed. For Rammohun Roy as for Bankimchandra Chattopadhyay, two of India's most prominent nationalist intellectuals of the nineteenth century, British rule was a necessary period of tutelage that Indians had to undergo in order to prepare precisely for what the British denied but extolled as the end of all history: citizenship and the nation state. Years later, in 1951, an "unknown" Indian who successfully sold his "obscurity" dedicated the story of his life thus:

To the memory of the
British Empire in India

Which conferred subjecthood on us
But withheld citizenship;
To which yet
Everyone of us threw out the challenge
"Civis Britanicus Sum"
Because
All that was good and living
Within us
Was made, shaped, and quickened
By the same British Rule.[14]

In nationalist versions of this narrative, as Partha Chatterjee has shown, it was the peasants and the workers, the subaltern classes, who were given to bear the cross of "inadequacy," for, according to this version, it was they who needed to be educated out of their ignorance, parochialism, or, depending on your preference, false consciousness.[15] Even today the Anglo-Indian word *communalism* refers to those who allegedly fail to measure up to the "secular" ideals of citizenship.

That British rule put in place the practices, institutions, and discourse of bourgeois individualism in the Indian soil is undeniable. Early expressions — that is, before the beginnings of nationalism — of this desire to be a "legal subject" make it clear that to Indians in the 1830s and 1840s to be a "modern individual" was to become a "European." *The Literary Gleaner*, a magazine in colonial Calcutta, ran the following poem in 1842, written in English by a Bengali schoolboy eighteen years of age. The poem apparently was inspired by the sight of ships leaving the coast of Bengal "for the glorious shores of England":

Oft like a sad bird I sigh
To leave this land, though mine own land it be;
Its green robed meads, — gay flowers and cloudless sky
Though passing fair, have but few charms for me.
For I have dreamed of climes more bright and free
Where virtue dwells and heaven-born liberty
Makes even the lowest happy; — where the eye
Doth sicken not to see man bend the knee
To sordid interest: — climes where science thrives,
And genius doth receive her guerdon meet;
Where man in his all his truest glory lives,
And nature's face is exquisitely sweet:
For those fair climes I heave the impatient sigh,
There let me live and there let me die.[16]

In its echoes of Milton and seventeenth-century English

radicalism, this is obviously a piece of colonial pastiche.[17] Michael Madhusudan Dutt, the young Bengali author of this poem, eventually realized the impossibility of being "European" and returned to Bengali literature to become one of our finest poets. Later Indian nationalists, however, abandoned such abject desire to be "Europeans" themselves. Nationalist thought was premised precisely on the assumed universality of the project of becoming individuals, on the assumption that "individual rights" and abstract "equality" were universals that could find home anywhere in the world, that one could be both an "Indian" and a "citizen" at the same time. We shall soon explore some of the contradictions of this project.

Many of the public and private rituals of modern individualism became visible in India in the nineteenth century. One sees this, for instance, in the sudden flourishing in this period of the four basic genres that help express the modern self: the novel, the biography, the autobiography, and history.[18] Along with these came modern industry, technology, medicine, a quasibourgeois (though colonial) legal system supported by a state that nationalism was to take over and make its own. The transition narrative that I have been discussing underwrote, and was in turn underpinned by, these institutions. To think this narrative was to think these institutions at the apex of which sat the modern state,[19] and to think the modern or the nation state was to think a history whose theoretical subject was Europe. Gandhi realized this as early as 1909. Referring to the Indian nationalists' demands for more railways, modern medicine, and bourgeois law, he cannily remarked in his book *Hind Swaraj* that this was to "make India English" or, as he put it, to have "English rule without the Englishman."[20] This "Europe," as Michael Madhusudan Dutt's youthful and naive poetry shows, was of course nothing but a piece of fiction told to the colonized by the colonizer in the very process of fabricating colonial domination[21] Gandhi's critique of this "Europe" is compromised on many points by his nationalism, and I do not intend to fetishize his text. But I find his gesture useful in developing the problematic of nonmetropolitan histories.

III

I shall now return to the themes of "failure," "lack," and "inadequacy" that so ubiquitously characterize the speaking subject of "Indian" history. As in the practice of the insurgent peasants of colonial India, the first step in a critical effort must arise from a gesture of inversion.[22] Let us begin from where the transition narrative ends and read "plenitude" and "creativity" where this narrative has made us read "lack" and "inadequacy."

According to the fable of their constitution, Indians today are all "citizens." The constitution embraces almost a classically liberal definition of citizenship. If the modern state and the modern individual, the citizen, are but the two inseparable sides of the same phenomenon, as William Connolly argues in *Political Theory and Modernity*, it would appear that the end of history is in sight for us in India.[23] This modern individual, however, whose political/public life is lived in citizenship, is also supposed to have an interiorized "private" self that pours out incessantly in diaries, letters, autobiographies, novels, and, of course, in what we say to our analysts. The bourgeois individual is not born until one discovers the pleasures of privacy. But this is a very special kind of "private" — it is, in fact, a deferred "public," for this bourgeois private, as Jürgen Habermas has reminded us, is "always already oriented to an audience [*Publikum*]." [24]

Indian public life may mimic on paper the bourgeois legal fiction of citizenship — the fiction is usually performed as a farce in India — but what about the bourgeois private and its history? Anyone who has tried to write "French" social history with Indian material would know how impossibly difficult the task is.[25] It is not that the form of the bourgeois private did not come with European rule. There have been, since the middle of the nineteenth century, Indian novels, diaries, letters, and autobiographies, but they seldom yield pictures of an endlessly interiorized subject. Our autobiographies are remarkably "public" (with constructions of public life that are not necessarily modern) when written by men, and they tell the story of the extended family when written by women.[26] In any case, autobiographies in the confessional mode are notable for their absence. The single paragraph (out of 963 pages) that Nirad Chaudhuri spends on describing the experience of his wedding night in the second volume of his celebrated and prize-winning autobiography is as good an example as any other and is worth quoting at some length. I should explain that this was an arranged marriage (Bengal, 1932), and Chaudhuri was anxious lest his wife should not appreciate his newly acquired but unaffordably expensive hobby of buying records of Western classical music. Our reading of Chaudhuri is handicapped in part by our lack of knowledge of the intertextuality of his prose — there may have been at work, for instance, an imbibed puritanical revulsion against revealing "too much." Yet the passage remains a telling exercise in the construction of memory, for it is about what Chaudhuri "remembers" and "forgets" of his "first night's experience." He screens off intimacy with expressions like "I do not remember" or "I do not know how" (not to mention the very Freudian "making a clean breast of"), and this self-constructed veil is no doubt a part of the self that speaks:

I was terribly uneasy at the prospect of meeting as wife a girl who was a complete stranger to me, and when she was brought in... and left standing before me I had nothing to say. I saw only a very shy smile on her face, and timidly she came and sat by my side on the edge of the bed. I do not know how after that both of us drifted to the pillows, to lie down side by side. [Chaudhuri adds in a footnote: "Of course, fully dressed. We Hindus... consider both extremes — fully clad and fully nude — to be modest, and everything in-between as grossly immodest. No decent man wants his wife to be an ***allumeuse****."] Then the first words were exchanged. She took up one of my arms, felt it and said: "You are so thin. I shall take good care of you." I did not thank her, and I do not remember that beyond noting the words I even felt touched. The horrible suspense about European music had reawakened in my mind, and I decided to make a clean breast of it at once and look the sacrifice, if it was called for, straight in the face and begin romance on such terms as were offered to me. I asked her timidly after a while: "Have you listened to any European music?" She shook her head to* *say "No." Nonetheless, I took another chance and this time asked: "Have you heard the name of a man called Beethoven?" She nodded and signified "Yes." I was reassured, but not wholly satisfied. So I asked yet again: "Can you spell the name?" She said slowly: "B, E, E, T, H, O,V, E, N." I felt very encouraged... and [we] dozed off.*[27]

The desire to be "modern" screams out of every sentence in the two volumes of Chaudhuri's autobiography. His legendary name now stands for the cultural history of Indo-British encounter. Yet in the 1500-odd pages that he has written in English about his life, this is the only passage where the narrative of Chaudhuri's participation in public life and literary circles is interrupted to make room for something approaching the intimate. How do we read this text, this self-making of an Indian male who was second to no one in his ardor for the public life of the citizen, yet who seldom, if ever, reproduced in writing the other side of the modern citizen, the interiorized private self unceasingly reaching out for an audience? Public without private? Yet another instance of the "incompleteness" of bourgeois transformation in India?

These questions are themselves prompted by the transition narrative that in turn situates the modern individual at the very end of history. I do not wish to confer on Chaudhuri's autobiography a representativeness it may not have. Women's writings, as I have already said, are different, and scholars have just begun to explore the world of autobiographies in Indian history. But if one result of European imperialism in India was to introduce the modern state and the idea of the nation with their attendant discourse of "citizenship," which, by the very idea of "the citizen's rights" (i.e., "the rule of law"), splits the figure of the modern individual into "public" and "private" parts of the self (as the young Marx once pointed out in his *On the Jewish Question*), these themes have existed — in contestation, alliance, and miscegenation — with other narratives of the self and community that do not look to the state/citizen bind as the ultimate construction of sociality.[28] This as such will not be disputed, but my point goes further. It is that these other constructions of self and community, while documentable in themselves, will never enjoy the privilege of providing the metanarratives or teleologies (assuming that there cannot be a narrative without at least an implicit teleology) of our histories. This is so partly because these narratives often themselves bespeak an antihistorical consciousness; that is, they entail subject positions and configurations of memory that challenge and undermine the subject that speaks in the name of history.

"History" is precisely the site where the struggle goes on to appropriate, on behalf of the modern (my hyperreal Europe), these other collocations of memory.

To illustrate these propositions, I will now discuss a fragment of this contested history in which the modern private and the modern individual were embroiled in colonial India.[29]

IV

What I present here are the outlines, so to speak, of a chapter in the history of bourgeois domesticity in colonial Bengal. The material-in the main texts produced in Bengali between 1850 and 1920 for teaching women that very Victorian subject, "domestic science" — relates to the Bengali Hindu middle class, the *bhadralok* or "respectable people." British rule instituted into Indian life the trichotomous ideational division on which modern political structures rest, e.g., the state, civil society, and the (bourgeois) family. It was therefore not surprising that ideas relating to bourgeois domesticity, privacy, and individuality should come to India via British rule. What I want to highlight here, however, through the example of the *bhadralok*, are certain cultural operations by which the "Indians" challenged and modified these received ideas in such a way as to put in question two fundamental tenets underlying the idea of "modernity" — the nuclear family based on companionate marriage and the secular, historical construction of time.

As Meredith Borthwick, Ghulam Murshid, and other scholars have shown, the eighteenth-century European idea of "civilization" culminated, in early nineteenth-century India, in a full-blown imperialist critique of Indian/Hindu domestic life, which was now held to be inferior to what became mid-Victorian ideals of The "condition of women" bourgeois domesticity.[30] question in nineteenth-century India was part of that critique, as were the ideas of the "modern" individual, "freedom," "equality," and "rights." In passages remarkable for their combination of egalitarianism and orientalism, James Mill's *The History of British India* (1817) joined together the thematic of the family/nation and a teleology of "freedom":

The condition of women is one of the most remarkable circumstances in the manners of nations... The history of uncultivated nations uniformly represents the women as in a state of abject slavery, from which they slowly emerge as civilisation advances... As society refines upon its enjoyments... the condition of the weaker sex is gradually improved, till they associate on equal terms with the men, and occupy the place of voluntary and useful coadjutors. A state of dependence more strict and humiliating than that which is ordained for the weaker sex among the Hindus cannot be easily conceived.[31]

As is well known, the Indian middle classes generally felt answerable to this charge. From the early nineteenth-century onward a movement developed in Bengal (and other regions) to reform "women's conditions" and to give them formal education. Much of this discourse on women's education was emancipationist in that it spoke the language of "freedom," "equality," and "awakening," and was strongly influenced by Ruskinian ideals and idealization of bourgeois domesticity.[32] If one looks on this history as part of the history of the modern individual in India, an interesting feature emerges. It is that in this literature on women's education certain terms, after all, were much more vigorously debated than others. There was, for example, a degree of consensus over the desirability of domestic "discipline" and "hygiene" as practices reflective of a state of modernity, but the word *freedom*, yet another important term in the rhetoric of the modern, hardly ever acted as the register of such a social consensus. It was a passionately disputed word, and we would be wrong to assume that the passions reflected a simple and straightforward battle of the sexes. The word was assimilated to the nationalist need to construct cultural boundaries that supposedly separated the "European" from the "Indian." The dispute over this word was thus central to the discursive strategies through which a subject position was created enabling the "Indian" to speak. It is this subject position that I want to discuss here in some detail.

What the Bengali literature on women's education played out was a battle between a nationalist construction of a cultural norm of the patriarchal, patrilocal, patrilineal extended family and the ideal of the patriarchal, bourgeois nuclear family that was implicit in the European/imperialist/universalist discourse on the "freedoms" of individualism, citizenship, and civil society.[33] The themes of "discipline" and "order" were critical in shaping nationalist imaginings of aesthetics and power. "Discipline" was seen as the key to the power of the colonial (i.e., modern) state, but it required certain procedures for redefining the self. The British were powerful, it was argued, because they were disciplined, orderly, and punctual in every detail of their lives, and this was made possible by the education of "their" women who brought the virtues of discipline into the home. The "Indian" home, a colonial construct, now fared badly in nationalist writings on modern domesticity. To quote a Bengali text on women's education from 1877:

*The house of any civilised European is like the abode of gods. Every household object is clean, set in its proper place and decorated; nothing seems unclean or smells foul... It is as if [the goddess of] order [**srinkhala**, "order, discipline"; **srinkhal**, "chains"] had become manifest to please the [human] eye. In the middle of the room would be a covered table with a bouquet of flowers on it, while around it would be [a few] chairs nicely arranged [with] everything sparkling clean. But enter a house in our country and you would feel as if you had been transported there by your destiny to make you atone for all the sins of your life. [A mass of] cowdung torturing the senses... dust in the air, a growing heap of ashes, flies buzzing around... a little boy urinating into the ground and putting the mess back into his mouth.... The whole place is dominated by a stench that seems to be running free... There is no order anywhere, the household objects are so unclean that they only evoke disgust.*[34]

This self-division of the colonial subject, the double movement of recognition by which it both knows its "present" as the site of disorder and yet moves away from this space in desiring a discipline that can only exist in an imagined but "historical" future, is a rehearsal, in the context of the discussion of the bourgeois domestic in colonial India, of the transition narrative we have encountered before. A historical construction of temporality (medieval/modern, separated by historical time), in other words, is precisely the axis along which the colonial subject splits itself. Or to put it differently, this split is what history is; writing history is performing this split over and over again.

The desire for order and discipline in the domestic sphere thus may be seen as having been a correlate of the nationalist, modernizing desire for a similar discipline in the public sphere, that is for a rule of law enforced by the state. It is beyond the scope of this paper to pursue this point further, but the connection between personal discipline and discipline in public life was to reveal itself in what the nationalists wrote about domestic hygiene and public health. The connection is recognizably modernist, and it is what the Indian modern shared with the European modern.[35] What I want to attend to, however, are the differences between the two. And this is where I turn to the other important aspect of the European modern, the rhetoric of "freedom" and "equality."

The argument about "freedom" — in the texts under discussion — was waged around the question of the Victorian ideals of the companionate marriage, that is, over the question as to whether or not the wife should also be a friend to the husband. Nothing threatened the ideal of the Bengali/Indian extended family (or the exalted position of the mother-in-law within that structure) more than this idea, wrapped up in notions of bourgeois privacy, that the wife was also to be a friend or, to put it differently, that the woman was now to be a modern individual. I must mention here that the modern individual, who asserts his/her individuality over the claims of the joint or extended family, almost always appears in nineteenth — and early twentieth-century Bengali literature as an embattled figure, often the subject of ridicule and scorn in the same Bengali fiction and essays that otherwise extolled the virtues of discipline and scientific rationality in personal and public lives. This irony had many expressions. The most well-known Bengali fictional character who represents this moral censure of modern individuality is Nimchand Datta in Dinabandhu Mitra's play *Sadhabar ekadashi* (1866). Nimchand, who is English-educated, quotes Shakespeare, Milton, or Locke at the slightest opportunity and uses this education arrogantly to ignore his duties toward his extended family, finds his nemeses in alcohol and debauchery. This metonymic relationship between the love of "modern"/English education (which stood for the romantic individual in nineteenth-century Bengal) and the slippery path of alcohol is suggested in the play by a conversation between

Nimchand and a Bengali official of the colonial bureaucracy, a Deputy Magistrate. Nimchand's supercilious braggadocio about his command of the English language quickly and inevitably runs to the subject of drinks (synonymous, in middle-class Bengali culture of the period, with absolute decadence):

I read English, write English, speechify in English, think in English, dream in English — mind you, it's no child's play — now tell me, my good fellow, what would you like to drink? — Claret for ladies, sherry for men and brandy for heroes.[36]

A similar connection between the modern, "free" individual and selfishness was made in the literature on women's education. The construction was undisguisedly nationalist (and patriarchal). *Freedom* was used to mark a difference between what was "Indian" and what was "European/English." The ultra-free woman acted like a *memsahib* (European woman), selfish and shameless. As Kundamala Devi, a woman writing for a women's magazine *Bamabodhini patrika*, said in 1870: "Oh dear ones! If you have acquired real knowledge, then give no place in your heart to *memsahib*-like behaviour. This is not becoming in a Bengali housewife."[37] The idea of "true modesty" was mobilized to build up this picture of the "really" Bengali woman.[38] Writing in 1920, Indira Devi dedicated her *Narir ukti* [A Woman Speaks] — interestingly enough, a defense of modern Bengali womanhood against criticisms by (predominantly) male writers — to generations of ideal Bengali women whom she thus described: "Unaffected by nature, of pleasant speech, untiring in their service [to others], oblivious of their own pleasures, [while] moved easily by the suffering of others, and capable of being content with very little."[39]

This model of the "modern" Bengali/Indian woman — educated enough to appreciate the modern regulations of the body and the state but yet "modest" enough to be unselfassertive and unselfish — was tied to the debates on "freedom." "Freedom" in the West, several authors argued, meant *jathechhachar*, to do as one pleased, the right to self-indulgence. In India, it was said, *freedom* meant freedom from the ego, the capacity to serve and obey voluntarily. Notice how the terms *freedom* and *slavery* have changed positions in the following quote:

To be able to subordinate oneself to others and to ***dharma*** *[duty/moral order/proper action]... to free the soul from the slavery of the senses, are the first tasks of human freedom. . . . That is why in Indian families boys and girls are subordinate* *to the parents, wife to the husband and to the parents-in-law, the disciple to the guru, the student to the teacher... the king to* ***dharma****... the people to the king, [and one's] dignity and prestige to [that of] the community [****samaj****].*[40]

There was an ironical twist to this theorizing that needs to be noted. Quite clearly, this theory of "freedom-in-obedience" did not apply to the domestic servants who were sometimes mentioned in this literature as examples of the "truly" unfree, the nationalist point being that (European) observers commenting on the unfree status of Indian women often missed (so some nationalists argued) this crucial distinction between the housewife and the domestic. Obviously, the servants were not yet included in the India of the nationalist imagination.

Thus went the Bengali discourse on modern domesticity in a colonial period when the rise of a civil society and a quasimodern state had already inserted the modern questions of "public" and "private" into middle-class Bengali lives. The received bourgeois ideas about domesticity and connections between the domestic and the national were modified here in two significant ways. One strategy, as I have sought to demonstrate, was to contrapose the cultural norm of the patriarchal extended family to the bourgeois patriarchal ideals of the companionate marriage, to oppose the new patriarchy with a redefined version of the old one(s). Thus was fought the idea of the modern private. The other strategy, equally significant, was to mobilize, on behalf of the extended family, forms and figurations of collective memory that challenged, albeit ambiguously, the seemingly absolute separation of "sacred" and "secular" time on which the very modern ("European") idea of history was/is based.[41] The figure of the "truly educated," "truly modest," and "truly Indian" woman is invested, in this discussion of women's education, with a sacred authority by subordinating the question of domestic life to religious ideas of female auspiciousness that joined the heavenly with the mundane in a conceptualization of time that could be only antihistorical. The truly modern housewife, it was said, would be so auspicious as to mark the eternal return of the cosmic principle embodied in the goddess Lakshmi, the goddess of domestic well-being by whose grace the extended family (and clan, and hence, by extending the sentiment, the nation, *Bharatlakshmi*) lived and prospered. Thus we read in a contemporary pamphlet: "Women are the Lakshmis of the community. If they undertake to improve themselves in the sphere of *dharma* and knowledge... there will be an automatic improvement in [the quality of] social life."[42] Lakshmi, regarded as the Hindu god Vishnu's wife by about

A.D. 400, has for long been held up in popular Hinduism, and in the everyday pantheism of Hindu families, as the model of the Hindu wife, united in complete harmony with her husband (and his family) through willful submission, loyalty, devotion, and chastity.[43] When women did not follow her ideals, it was said, the (extended) family and the family line were destroyed by the spirit of Alakshmi (not-Lakshmi), the dark and malevolent reverse of the Lakshmi principle. While women's education and the idea of discipline as such were seldom opposed in this discourse regarding the modern individual in colonial Bengal, the line was drawn at the point where modernity and the demand for bourgeois privacy threatened the power and the pleasures of the extended family.

There is no question that the speaking subject here is nationalist and patriarchal, employing the cliched orientalist categories, "the East" and "the West."[44] However, of importance to us are the two denials on which this particular moment of subjectivity rests: the denial, or at least contestation, of the bourgeois private and, equally important, the denial of historical time by making the family a site/where the sacred and the secular blended in a perpetual reenactment of a principle that was heavenly and divine.

The cultural space the antihistorical invoked was by no

means harmonious or nonconflictual, though nationalist thought of necessity tried to portray it to be so. The antihistorical norms of the patriarchal extended family, for example, could only have had a contested existence, contested both by women's struggles and by those of the subaltern classes. But these struggles did not necessarily follow any lines that would allow us to construct emancipatory narratives by putting the "patriarchals" clearly on one side and the "liberals" on the other. The history of modern "Indian" individuality is caught up in too many contradictions to lend itself to such a treatment.

I do not have the space here to develop the point, so I will make do with one example. It comes from the autobiography of Ramabai Ranade, the wife of the famous nineteenth-century social reformer from the Bombay Presidency, M. G. Ranade. Ramabai Ranade's struggle for self-respect was in part against the "old" patriarchal order of the extended family and for the "new" patriarchy of companionate marriage, which her reform-minded husband saw as the most civilized form of the conjugal bond. In pursuit of this ideal, Ramabai began to share her husband's commitment to public life and would often take part (in the 1880s) in public gatherings and deliberations of male and female social reformers. As she herself says: "It was at these meetings that I learnt what a meeting was and how one should conduct oneself at one."[45] Interestingly, however, one of the chief sources of opposition to Ramabai's efforts were (apart from men) the other women in the family. There is of course no doubt that they, her mother-in-law and her husband's sisters, spoke for the old patriarchal extended family. But it is quite instructive to listen to their voices (as they come across through Ramabai's text), for they also spoke for their own sense of self-respect and their own forms of struggle against men:

You should not really go to these meetings [they said to Ramabai]... Even if the men want you to do these things, you should ignore them. You need not say no: but after all, you need not do it. They will then give up, out of sheer boredom... You are outdoing even the European women.

Or this:

It is she [Ramabai] herself who loves this frivolousness of going to meetings. Dada [Mr. Ranade] is not at all so keen about it. But should she not have some sense of proportion of how much the women should actually do? If men tell you to do a hundred things, women should take up ten at the most. After all men do not understand these practical things! ... The good woman [in the past] never turned frivolous like this... That is why this large family... could live together in a respectable way... But now it is all so different! If Dada suggests one thing, this woman is prepared to do three. How can we live with any sense of self-respect then and how can we endure all this? (84-85)

These voices, combining the contradictory themes of nationalism, of patriarchal clan-based ideology, of women's struggles against men, and opposed at the same time to friendship between husbands and wives, remind us of the deep ambivalences that marked the trajectory of the modern private and bourgeois individuality in colonial India. Yet historians manage, by maneuvers reminiscent of the old "dialectical" card trick called "negation of negation," to deny a subject position to this voice of ambivalence. The evidence of what I have called "the denial of the bourgeois private and of the historical subject" is acknowledged but subordinated in their accounts to the supposedly higher purpose of making Indian history look like yet another episode in the universal and (in their view, the ultimately victorious) march of citizenship, of the nation state, of themes of human emancipation spelled out in the course of the European Enlightenment and after. It is the figure of the citizen that speaks through these histories. And so long as that happens, my hyperreal Europe will continually return to dominate the stories we tell. "The modern" will then continue to be understood, as Meaghan Morris has so aptly put it in discussing her own Australian context, "as a *known history*, something which has *already happened elsewhere*, and which is to be reproduced, mechanically or otherwise, with a local content." This can only leave us with a task of reproducing what Morris calls "the project of positive unoriginality."[46]

V

Yet the "originality" — I concede that this is a bad term — of the idioms through which struggles have been conducted in the Indian subcontinent has often been in the sphere of the nonmodern. One does not have to subscribe to the ideology of clannish patriarchy, for instance, to acknowledge that the metaphor of the sanctified and patriarchal extended family was one of the most important elements in the cultural politics of Indian nationalism. In the struggle against British rule, it was frequently the use of this idiom — in songs, poetry, and other forms of nationalist mobilization — that allowed "Indians" to fabricate a sense of community and to retrieve for themselves a subject position from which to address the British. I will illustrate this with an example from the life of Gandhi, "the father of the nation," to highlight the political importance of this cultural move on the part of the "Indian."

My example refers to the year 1946. There had been ghastly riots between the Hindus and the Muslims in Calcutta over the impending partition of the country into India and Pakistan. Gandhi was in the city, fasting in protest over the behavior of his own people. And here is how an Indian intellectual recalls the experience:

Men would come back from their offices in the evening and find food prepared by the family [meaning the womenfolk] ready for them; but soon it would be revealed that the women of the home had not eaten the whole day. They [apparently] had not felt hungry. Pressed further, the wife or the mother would admit that they could not understand how they could go on [eating] when Gandhiji was dying for their own crimes. Restaurants and amusement centres did little business; some of them were voluntarily closed by the proprietors... The nerve of feeling had been restored; the pain began to be felt... Gandhiji knew when to start the redemptive process.[47]

We do not have to take this description literally, but the nature of the community imagined in these lines is clear. It blends, in Gayatri Spivak's words, "the feeling of community that belongs to national links and political organizations" with "that other feeling of community whose structural model is the [clan or the extended] family."[48] Colonial Indian history is replete with instances where Indians arrogated subjecthood to themselves precisely by mobilizing, within the context of "modern" institutions and sometimes on behalf of the modernizing project of nationalism, devices of collective memory that were both antihistorical and antimodern.[49] This is not to deny the capacity of "Indians" to act as subjects endowed with what we in the universities would recognize as "a sense of history" (what Peter Burke calls "the renaissance of the past") but to insist at the same time that there were also contrary trends, that in the multifarious struggles that took place in colonial India, antihistorical constructions of the past often provided very powerful forms of collective memory.[50]

There is then this double bind through which the subject of "Indian" history articulates itself. On the one hand, it is both the subject and the object of modernity, because it stands for an assumed unity called the "Indian people" that is always split into two — a modernizing elite and a yet-to-be-modernized peasantry. As such a split subject, however, it speaks from within a metanarrative that celebrates the nation state; and of this metanarrative the theoretical subject can only be a hyperreal "Europe," a "Europe" constructed by the tales that both imperialism and nationalism have told the colonized. The mode of self-representation that the "Indian" can adopt here is what Homi Bhabha has justly called "mimetic."[51] Indian history, even in the most dedicated socialist or nationalist hands, remains a mimicry of a certain "modern" subject of "European" history and is bound to represent a sad figure of lack and failure. The transition narrative will always remain "grievously incomplete."

On the other hand, maneuvers are made within the space of the mimetic — and therefore within the project called "Indian" history — to represent the "difference" and the "originality" of the "Indian," and it is in this cause that the antihistorical devices of memory and the antihistorical "histories" of the subaltern classes are appropriated. Thus peasant/worker constructions of "mythical" kingdoms and "mythical" pasts/futures find a place in texts designated "Indian" history precisely through a procedure that subordinates these narratives to the rules of evidence and to the secular, linear calendar that the writing of "history" must follow. The antihistorical, antimodern subject, therefore, cannot speak itself as "theory" within the knowledge procedures of the university even when these knowledge procedures acknowledge and "document" its existence. Much like Spivak's "subaltern" (or the anthropologist's peasant who can only have a quoted existence in a larger statement that belongs to the anthropologist alone), this subject can only be spoken for and spoken of by the transition narrative that will always ultimately privilege the modern (i.e., "Europe").[52]

So long as one operates within the discourse of "history" produced at the institutional site of the university, it is not possible simply to walk out of the deep collusion between "history" and the modernizing narrative(s) of citizenship, bourgeois public and private, and the nation state. "History" as a knowledge system is firmly embedded in institutional practices that invoke the nation state at every step — witness the organization and politics of teaching, recruitment, promotions, and publication in history departments, politics that survive the occasional brave and heroic attempts by individual historians to liberate "history" from the metanarrative of the nation state. One only has to ask, for instance: Why is history a compulsory part of education of the modern person in all countries today including those that did quite comfortably without it until as late as the eighteenth century? Why should children all over the world today have to come to terms with a subject called "history" when we know that this compulsion is neither natural nor ancient?[53] It does not take much imagination to see that the reason for this lies in what European imperialism and third-world nationalisms have achieved together: the universalization of the nation state as the most desirable form of political community. Nation states have the capacity to enforce their truth games, and universities, their critical distance notwithstanding, are part of the battery of institutions complicit in this process. "Economics" and "history" are the knowledge forms that correspond to the two major institutions that the rise (and later universalization) of the bourgeois order has given to the world — the capitalist mode of production and the nation state ("history" speaking to the figure of the citizen).[54] A critical historian has no choice but to negotiate this knowledge. She or he therefore needs to understand the state on its own terms, i.e., in terms of its self-justificatory narratives of citizenship and modernity. Since these themes will always take us back to the universalist propositions of "modern" (European) political philosophy — even the "practical" science of economics that now seems "natural" to our constructions of world systems is (theoretically) rooted in the ideas of ethics in eighteenth-century Europe[55] — a third-world historian is condemned to knowing "Europe" as the original home of the "modern," whereas the "European" historian does not share a comparable predicament with regard to the pasts of the majority of humankind. Thus follows the everyday subalternity of non-Western histories with which I began this paper.

Yet the understanding that "we" all do "European" history with our different and often non-European archives opens up the possibility of a politics and project of alliance between the dominant metropolitan histories and the subaltern peripheral pasts. Let us call this the project of provincializing "Europe," the "Europe" that modern imperialism and (third-world) nationalism have, by their collaborative venture and violence, made universal. Philosophically, this project must ground itself in a radical critique and transcendence of liberalism (i.e., of the bureaucratic constructions of citizenship, modern state, and bourgeois privacy that classical political philosophy has produced), a ground that late Marx shares with certain moments in both poststructuralist thought and feminist philosophy. In particular, I am emboldened by Carole Pateman's courageous declaration — in her remarkable book *The Sexual Contract* — that the very conception of the modern individual belongs to patriarchal categories of thought.[56]

VI

The project of provincializing "Europe" refers to a history that does not yet exist; I can therefore only speak of it in a programmatic manner. To forestall misunderstanding, however, I must spell out what it is not while outlining what it could be.

To begin with, it does not call for a simplistic, out-of-hand rejection of modernity, liberal values, universals, science, reason, grand narratives, totalizing explanations, and so on. Fredric Jameson has recently reminded us that the easy equation often made between "a philosophical conception of totality" and "a political practice of totalitarianism" is "baleful."[57] What intervenes between the two is history — contradictory, plural, and heterogeneous struggles whose outcomes are never predictable, even retrospectively, in accordance with schemas that seek to naturalize and domesticate this heterogeneity. These struggles include coercion (both on behalf of and against modernity) — physical, institutional, and symbolic violence, often dispensed with dreamy-eyed idealism — and it is this violence that plays a decisive role in the establishment of meaning, in the creation of truth games, in deciding, as it were, whose and which "universal" wins. As intellectuals operating in academia, we are not neutral to these struggles and cannot pretend to situate ourselves outside of the knowledge procedures of our institutions.

The project of provincializing "Europe" therefore cannot be a project of "cultural relativism." It cannot originate from the stance that the reason/science/universals which help define Europe as the modern are simply "culture-specific" and therefore only belong to the European cultures. For the point is not that Enlightenment rationalism is always unreasonable in itself but rather a matter of documenting how — through what historical process — its "reason," which was not always self-evident to everyone, has been made to look "obvious" far beyond the ground where it originated. If a language, as has been said, is but a dialect backed up by an army, the same could be said of the narratives of "modernity" that, almost universally today, point to a certain "Europe" as the primary habitus of the modern.

This Europe, like "the West," is demonstrably an imaginary entity, but the demonstration as such does not lessen its appeal or power. The project of provincializing "Europe" has to include certain other additional moves: 1) the recognition that Europe's acquisition of the adjective *modern* for itself is a piece of global history of which an integral part is the story of European imperialism; and 2) the understanding that this equating of a certain version of Europe with "modernity" is not the work of Europeans alone; third-world nationalisms, as modernizing ideologies *par excellence*, have been equal partners in the process. I do not mean to overlook the anti-imperial moments in the careers of these nationalisms; I only underscore the point that the project of provincializing "Europe" cannot be a nationalist, nativist, or atavistic project. In unraveling the necessary entanglement of history — a disciplined and institutionally regulated form of collective memory — with the grand narratives of "rights," "citizenship," the nation state, "public" and "private" spheres, one cannot but problematize "India" at the same time as one dismantles "Europe."

The idea is to write into the history of modernity the ambivalences, contradictions, the use of force, and the tragedies and the ironies that attend it. That the rhetoric and the claims of (bourgeois) equality, of citizens' rights, of self-determination through a sovereign nation state have in many circumstances empowered marginal social groups in their struggles is undeniable — this recognition is indispensable to the project of *Subaltern Studies*. What effectively is played down, however, in histories that either implicitly or explicitly celebrates the advent of the modern state and the idea of citizenship is the repression and violence that are as instrumental in the victory of the modern as is the persuasive power of its rhetorical strategies. Nowhere is this irony — the undemocratic foundations of "democracy" — more visible than in the history of modern medicine, public health, and personal hygiene, the discourses of which have been central in locating the body of the modern at the intersection of the public and the private (as defined by, and subject to negotiations with, the state). The triumph of this discourse, however, has always been dependent on the mobilization, on its behalf, of effective means of physical coercion. I say "always" because this coercion is both originary/foundational (i.e., historic) as well as pandemic and quotidian. Of foundational violence, David Arnold gives a good example in a recent essay on the history of the prison in India. The coercion of the colonial prison, Arnold shows, was integral to some of the earliest and pioneering research on the medical, dietary, and demographic statistics of India, for the prison was where Indian bodies were accessible to modernizing investigators.[58] Of the coercion that continues in the names of the nation and modernity, a recent example comes from the Indian campaign to eradicate smallpox in the 1970s. Two American doctors (one of them presumably of "Indian" origin) who participated in the process thus describe their operations in a village of the Ho tribe in the Indian state of Bihar:

In the middle of gentle Indian night, an intruder burst through the bamboo door of the simple adobe hut. He was a government vaccinator, under orders to break resistance against smallpox vaccination. Lakshmi Singh awoke screaming and scrambled to hide herself. Her husband leaped out of bed, grabbed an axe, and chased the intruder into the courtyard. Outside a squad of doctors and policemen quickly overpowered Mohan Singh. The instant he was pinned to the ground, a second vaccinator jabbed smallpox vaccine into his arm. Mohan Singh, a wiry 40-year-old leader of the Ho tribe, squirmed away from the needle, causing the vaccination site to bleed. The government team held him until they had injected enough vaccine... While the two policemen rebuffed him, the rest of the team overpowered the entire family and vaccinated each in turn. Lakshmi Singh bit deep into one doctor's hand, but to no avail.[59]

There is no escaping the idealism that accompanies this violence. The subtitle of the article in question unselfconsciously reproduces both the military and the do-gooding instincts of the enterprise. It reads: "How an army of samaritans drove smallpox from the earth."

Histories that aim to displace a hyperreal Europe from the center toward which all historical imagination currently gravitates will have to seek out relentlessly this connection between violence and idealism that lies at the heart of the process by which the narratives of citizenship and modernity come to find a natural home in "history." I register a fundamental disagreement here with a position taken by Richard Rorty in an exchange with Jürgen Habermas. Rorty criticizes Habermas for the latter's conviction "that the story of modern philosophy is an important part of the story of the democratic societies' attempts at self-reassurance."[60] Rorty's statement follows the practice of many Europeanists who speak of the histories of these "democratic societies" as if these were self-contained histories complete in themselves, as if the self-fashioning of the West were something that occurred only within its self-assigned geographical boundaries. At the very least Rorty ignores the role that the "colonial theater" (both external and internal) — where the theme of "freedom" as defined by modern political philosophy was constantly invoked in aid of the ideas of "civilization," "progress," and latterly "development" — played in the process of engendering this "reassurance." The task, as I see it, will be to wrestle ideas that legitimize the modern state and its attendant institutions, in order to return to political philosophy — in the same way as suspect coins returned to their owners in an Indian bazaar — its categories whose global currency can no longer be taken for granted.[61]

And, finally — since "Europe" cannot after all be provincialized within the institutional site of the university whose knowledge protocols will always take us back to the terrain where all contours follow that of my hyperreal Europe — the project of provincializing Europe must realize within itself its own impossibility. It therefore looks to a history that embodies this politics of despair. It will have been clear by now that this is not a call for cultural relativism or for atavistic, nativist histories. Nor is this a program for a simple rejection of modernity, which would be, in many situations, politically suicidal. I ask for a history that deliberately makes visible, within the very structure of its narrative forms, its own repressive strategies and practices, the part it plays in collusion with the narratives of citizenships in assimilating to the projects of the modern state all other possibilities of human solidarity. The politics of despair will require of such history that it lays bare to its readers the reasons why such a predicament is necessarily inescapable. This is a history that will attempt the impossible: to look toward its own death by tracing that which resists and escapes the best human effort at translation across cultural and other semiotic systems, so that the world may once again be imagined as radically heterogeneous. This, as I have said, is impossible within the knowledge protocols of academic history, for the globality of academia is not independent of the globality that the European modern has created. To attempt to provincialize this "Europe" is to see the modern as inevitably contested, to write over the given and privileged narratives of citizenship other narratives of human connections that draw sustenance from dreamed-up pasts and futures where collectivities are defined neither by the rituals of citizenship nor by the nightmare of "tradition" that "modernity" creates. There are of course no (infra)structural sites where such dreams could lodge themselves. Yet they will recur so long as the themes of citizenship and the nation state dominate our narratives of historical transition, for these dreams are what the modern represses in order to be.

Notes

Many different audiences in the United States and Australia have responded to versions of this paper and helped me with their criticisms. My benefactors are too numerous to mention individually but the following have been particularly helpful: the editorial board of Representations for criticisms conveyed through Thomas Laqueur, Benedict Anderson, Arjun Appadurai, David Arnold, Marjorie Beale, Partha Chatterjee, Natalie Davis, Nicholas Dirks, Simon During, John Foster, Ranajit Guha, Jeanette Hoorn, Martin Jay, Jenny Lee, David Lloyd, Fiona Nicoll, Gyanendra Pandey, Craig Reynolds, Joan Scott, and Gayatri Spivak. And very special thanks to Christopher Healy for sharing both the intellectual and the physical labor that went into this paper.

Endnotes:

1. Ranajit Guha and Gayatri Chakravorty Spivak, eds., *Selected Subaltern Studies* (New York, 1988); Ronald Inden, "Orientalist Constructions of India," *Modern Asian Studies* 20, no. 3 (1986): 445.

2. I am indebted to Jean Baudrillard for the term *hyperreal* (see his *Simulations* [New York, 1983]), but my use differs from his.

3. Linda Hutcheon, *The Politics of Postmodernism* (London, 1989), 65.

4. Edmund Husserl, *The Crisis of European Sciences and Transcendental Philosophy*, trans. David Carr (Evanston, Ill., 1970), 281-85. See also Wilhelm Halbfass, *India and Europe: An Essay in Understanding* (New York, 1988), 167-68.

5. See the discussion in Karl Marx, *Grundrisse: Foundations of the Critique of Political Economy*, trans. Martin Nicholas (Harmondsworth, Eng., 1973), 469-512; and in Marx, *Capital: A Critique of Political Economy,* 3 vols. (Moscow, 1971), 3: 593-613.

6. See Dipesh Chakrabarty, *Rethinking Working-Class History: Bengal,* 1890-1940 (Princeton, N.J., 1989), chap. 7.

7. Marx, *Capital*, 1:60.

8. Marx, *Grundrisse*, 105.

9. See Chakrabarty, *Rethinking Working-Class History*, chap. 7, in particular.

10. Sumit Sarkar, *Modern India*, 1885-1947 (Delhi, 1985), 1.

11. Guha and Spivak, *Selected Subaltern Studies*, 43. The words quoted here are Guha's. But I think they represent a sense of historiographical responsibility that is shared by all the members of the Subaltern Studies collective.

12. Alexander Dow, *History of Hindostan*, 3 vols. (London, 1812-16), dedication, vol. 1.

13. See L. T. Hobhouse, *Liberalism* (New York, 1964), 26-27.

14. Nirad C. Chaudhuri, *The Autobiography of an Unknown Indian* (New York, 1989), dedication page.

15. Partha Chatterjee, *Nationalist Thought and the Colonial World: A Derivative Discourse?* (London, 1986).

16. *Mudhusudan rachanabali* [Bengali] (Calcutta, 1965), 449. See also Jogindranath Basu, *Michael Madhusudan Datter jibancharit* [Bengali] (Calcutta, 1978), 86.

17. My understanding of this poem has been enriched by discussions with Marjorie Levinson and David Bennett.

18. I am not making the claim that all of these genres necessarily emerge with bourgeois individualism. See Natalie Zemon Davis, "Fame and Secrecy: Leon Modena's *Life* as an Early Modern Autobiography," *History and Theory* 27 (1988): 103-18; and Davis, "Boundaries and Sense of Self in Sixteenth-Century France," in Thomas C. Heller et al., eds., *Reconstructing Individualism: Autonomy, Individuality, and the Self in Western Thought* (Stanford, Calif., 1986), 53-63. See also Philippe Lejeune, *On Autobiography*, trans. Katherine Leary (Minneapolis, 1989), 163-84.

19. See the chapter on Nehru in Chatterjee, *Nationalist Thought*.

20. M. K. Gandhi, *Hindswaraj* (1909), in *Collected Works ofMahatma Gandhi*, vol. 10 (Ahmedabad, 1963), 15.

21. See the discussion in Gauri Visvanathan, *Masks of Conquest: Literary Studies and British Rule in India* (London, 1989), 128-41, passim.

22. Ranajit Guha, *Elementary Aspects of Peasant Insurgency in Colonial India* (New Delhi, 1983), chap. 2.

23. William E. Connolly, *Political Theory and Modernity* (Oxford, 1989). See also David Bennett, "Postmodernism and Vision: Ways of Seeing (at) the End of History" (forthcoming).

24. Jiirgen Habermas, *The Structural Transformation of the Public Sphere: An Inquiry into a Category ofBourgeois Society* (Cambridge, Mass., 1989), 49.

25. See Sumit Sarkar, "Social History: Predicament and Possibilities," in Iqbal Khan, ed., *Fresh Perspective on India and Pakistan: Essays on Economics, Politics, and Culture* (Oxford, 1985), 256-74.

26. For reasons of space, I shall leave this claim here unsubstantiated, though I hope to have an opportunity to discuss it in detail elsewhere. I should qualify the statement by mentioning that in the main it refers to autobiographies published between 1850 and 1910. Once women join the public sphere in the twentieth century, their selffashioning takes on different dimensions.

27. Nirad C. Chaudhuri, *Thy Hand, Great Anarch!: India*, 1921-1952 (London, 1987), 350-51.

28. See Karl Marx, On the Jewish Question, in *Early Writings* (Harmondsworth, Eng., 1975), 215-22.

29. For a more detailed treatment of what follows, see my paper "Colonial Rule and the Domestic Order," to be published in David Arnold and David Hardiman, eds., *Subaltern Studies*, vol. 8.

30. Meredith Borthwick, *The Changing Role of Women in Bengal,* 1849-1905 (Princeton, N.J., 1984); Ghulam Murshid, Reluctant Debutante: *Response of Bengali Women to Modernisation*, 1849-1905 (Rajshahi, 1983). On the history of the word *civilization*, see Lucien Febvre, "*Civilisation*: Evolution of a Word and a Group of Ideas," in Peter Burke, ed., *A New Kind of History: From the Writings of Febvre*, trans. K. Folca (London, 1973), 219-57. I owe this reference to Peter Sahlins.

31. James Mill, *The History of British India*, vol. 1, ed. H. H. Wilson (London, 1840), 309-10.

32. Borthwick, *Changtng Role*.

33. The classic text where this assumption has been worked up into philosophy is of course *Hegel's Philosophy of Right*, trans. T.M. Knox (Oxford, 1967), 110-22. See also Joanna Hodge, "Women and the Hegelian State," in Ellen Kennedy and Susan Mendus, eds., *Women in Western Philosophy* (Brighton, Eng., 1987), 127-58; Simon During, "Rousseau's Heirs: Primitivism, Romance, and Other Relations Between the Modern and the Nonmodern" (forthcoming); Joan B. Landes, *Women and the Public Sphere in the Age of the French Revolution* (Ithaca, N.Y., 1988); Mary Ryan, *Women in Public: Between Banners and Ballots*, 1825-1880 (Baltimore, 1990).

34. Anon., *Streesiksha*, vol. 1 (Calcutta, 1877), 28-29.

35. I develop this argument further in Dipesh Chakrabarty, "Open Space/Public Place: Garbage, Modernity, and India," *South Asia* (forthcoming).

36. *Dinabandhu racanabali*, ed. Kshetra Gupta (Calcutta, 1981), 138.

37. Borthwick, *Changing Role*, 105.

38. I discuss this in more detail in Chakrabarty, "Colonial Rule."

39. Indira Devi, *Narir ukti* (Calcutta, 1920), dedication page.

40. Deenanath Bandyopadhyaya, *Nanabishayak prabandha* (Calcutta, 1887), 30-31. For a genealogy of the terms *slavery* and *freedom* as used in the colonial discourse of British India, see Cyan Prakash, *Bonded Histories: Genealogies of Labor Servitude in Colonial India* (Cambridge, 1990).

41. Peter Burke, *The Renaissance Sense of the Past* (London, 1970).

42. Bikshuk [Chandrasekhar Sen], *Ki holo!* (Calcutta, 1876), 77.

43. David Kinsley, *Hindu Goddesses: Visions of the Divine Feminine in the Hindu Religious Tradition* (Berkeley, 1988), 19-31; Manomohan Basu, *Hindu acar byabahar* (Calcutta, 1873), 60; H. D. Bhattacharya, "Minor Religious Sects," in R. C. Majumdar, ed., *The History and Culture of the Indian People: The Age of Imperial Unity*, vol. 2 (Bombay, 195

1), 469-71; Upendranath Dhal, *Goddess Lakshmi: Origin and Development* (Delhi, 1978). The *expression everyday* pantheism was suggested to me by Gayatri Chakravorty Spivak (personal communication).

44. See the chapter on Bankim in Chatterjee, *Nationalist Thought.*

45. *Ranade: His Wife's Reminiscences,* trans. Kusumavati Deshpande (Delhi, 1963), 77.

46. Meaghan Morris, "Metamorphoses at Sydney Tower," *New Formations* 11 (Summer 1990): 10.

47. Amiya Chakravarty, quoted in Bhikhu Parekh, *Gandhi's Political Discourse* (London, 1989), 163.

48. Gayatri Chakravorty Spivak, "Can the Subaltern Speak?," in Cary Nelson and Lawrence Grossberg, eds., *Marxism and the Interpretation of Culture* (Urbana, Ill., 1988), 277.

49. See *Subaltern Studies*, vols. 1-7 (Delhi, 1982-91); and Ashis Nandy, *The Intimate Enemy: Loss and Recovery of Self Under* Colonialism (Delhi, 1983).

50. *Subaltern Studies*, vols. 1-7, and Guha, *Elementary Aspects.*

51. Horni Bhabha, "Of Mimicry and Man: The Ambivalence of Colonial Discourse," in Annette Michelson et al., eds., *October: The First Decade*, 1976-1986 (Cambridge, Mass., 1987), 317-26; also Bhabha, ed., *Nation and Narration* (London, 1990).

52. Spivak, "Can the Subaltern Speak?" Also see Spivak's interview published in Socialist Review 20, no. 3 (July-September 1990): 81-98.

53. On the close connection between imperialist ideologies and the teaching of history in colonial India, see Ranajit Guha, *An Indian Historiography of India: A Nineteenth-Century Agenda and Its Implications* (Calcutta, 1988).

54. Without in any way implicating them in the entirety of this argument, I may mention that there are parallels here between my statement and what Gyan Prakash and Nicholas Dirks have argued elsewhere. See Gyan Prakash, "Writing Post-Orientalist Histories of the

Third World: Perspectives from Indian Historiography," *Comparative Studies in Society and History* 32, no. 2 (April 1990): 383-408; Nicholas B. Dirks, "History as a Sign of the Modern," *Public Culture* 2, no. 2 (Spring 1990): 25-33.

55. See Amartya Kumar Sen, *Of Ethics and Economics* (Oxford, 1987). Tessa Morris-Suzuki's *A History of Japanese Economic Thought* (London, 1989) makes interesting reading in this regard. I am grateful to Gavan McCormack for bringing this book to my attention.

56. Carole Pateman, *The Sexual Contract* (Stanford, Calif., 1988), 184.

57. Fredric Jameson, "Cognitive Mapping," in Nelson and Grossberg, *Marxism and the Interpretation of Culture*, 354.

58. David Arnold, "The Colonial Prison: Power, Knowledge, and Penology in Nineteenth-Century India," in Arnold and Hardiman, *Subaltern Studies*, vol. 8. I have discussed some of these issues in a Bengali article: Dipesh Chakrabarty, "Sarir, samaj, o rashtra: Oupanibeshik bharate mahamari o janasangskriti," *Anustup*, 1988.

59. Lawrence Brilliant with Girija Brilliant, "Death for a Killer Disease," *Quest*, May/June 1978, 3. I owe this reference to Paul Greenough.

60. Richard Rorty, "Habermas and Lyotard on Postmodernity," in Richard J. Bernstein, ed., *Habermas and Modernity* (Cambridge, Mass., 1986), 169.

61. For an interesting and revisionist reading of Hegel in this regard, see the exchange between Charles Taylor and Partha Chatterjee in *Public Culture* 3, no. 1 (1990). My book *Rethinking Working-Class History* attempts a small beginning in this direction.

Museums in Late Democracies

Two Models of Democracy

Before I get on to the matter of museums and their evolving relationship to democracies—my real subject in this short and sketchy essay — let me begin by explaining briefly what I see as the two models of democracy that coexist and sometimes clash in contemporary democratic polities. In the interest of brevity and exposition, I will keep my models separate and simple. Nineteenth and early twentieth-century ideas of democracy assumed a pedagogical understanding of politics. One was never born political even if it were thought that every human being had the capacity or the potential to take part in political life. But the condition of being human was not equated to the condition of being political. It was assumed that becoming a citizen, possessing and exercising rights, called for appropriate forms of education. Societies were understood to have both high and low forms of culture. Education provided the capacity for discernment — access to high culture — that the citizen needed. This could be self-education. It could be education through the right kind of experience. More commonly, however, it was thought that it fell to the educational institutions of modern societies to provide citizenly competence. Universities, museums, libraries, exhibitions and other comparable bodies assumed this task.[1] A crucial aspect of this education was the capacity for abstract conceptualisation and reasoning. The book became the key object embodying this assumption. The importance given to the written language as the medium of instruction signified the high place accorded in this mode of thought to the trained, human capacity for abstraction. Abstract reasoning made it possible for the citizen to conceptualise such imaginary\entities as "*class*", "*public*", or "*national*" interest and adjudicate between competing claims. Rationality was not merely a procedural aspect of disputations in life; it was itself thought to be an instrument of unity in public discussions. Rationality could help us appreciate our interests and arrange them mentally in the right order of priority. The public sphere was not only imagined as potentially united and unifiable; such unity was itself a value. For Marxists, "class" could be the rational key explaining and promoting a unity between diverse underprivileged groups. For nationalists, something like "national interest" could be a factor that overrode all divisions born of sectional interests. For liberals, rationality could lead to appreciation of that which was in the interest of all. Expanding the area of agreement through education and rational argumentation was seen as way of strengthening the fabric of national life.

This pedagogical understanding of citizenship is not

history. It is not something we have left behind. Many of our institutional and personal actions are based on this understanding. Yet twentieth-century practices of mass-democracy — both in the West and in countries such as India — are also predicated on a very different understanding of the political. Following Homi Bhabha's usage of the terms "pedagogic" and "performative," we may call the second model of democratic politics a "performative" one.[2] The political, in this model, is not fundamentally a matter of pedagogy. The citizen is not someone who comes or is produced at the end of an educational process in which the school, the university, the library, and the museum intervene. In this conception that has increasingly dominated debates in and about public life in democracies since the 1960s, to be human is to be already political. Statements such as "everything is political," or "the personal is political" are reflections of this point of view. An Australian example will illustrate my point about the difference between the two models of democracy. A. P. Elkin, Professor of Anthropology at the University of Sydney from 1934 to 1956, advocated citizenship for Aboriginals but supported only "a gradual granting" of such rights. Only "civilised" Aboriginals, according to him, were fit for citizenship.[3] Elkin, in my terms, stood for the first model. Yet when Aboriginals finally obtained (partial) citizenship in 1967, the decision obviously did not reflect Elkin's position.[4] Any Aboriginal, formally educated or not, was now seen as entitled to the rights of the citizen. The same point could be made with respect to the Indian decision, on the attainment of independence, to adopt universal adult franchise as a citizenly right in a society that was predominantly non-literate. This was part of a global trend the beginnings of which can be traced back at least as far as the 1920s when the fear of Bolshevism, for example, induced Western governments to extend to working classes in many countries the rights of organisation and protest. The acquisition of these rights was no longer made conditional on any preparatory work on behalf of the people. In short, the pedagogical or tutelage model of politics simply could not keep pace with the speed with which the world got politicised last century. The Soviet revolution, anti-colonial mass nationalisms in the non-West, and emergence of mass politics in the West were important contributors to the process until the 1950s. And then came the "new" social movements and counter-cultural movements of the 1960s, first-wave feminism with its slogan "the personal is political", and the politics of multiculturalism and indigenous rights in the Western democracies. The spread of consumerism and the mass media has been an inextricable part of this search for forms of mass democracy. For the rise of the mass-consumer and the question of his or her rights — a growing concern of capitalist democracies — entailed both understandings of the political. The consumer is a subject of pedagogy. She or he is routinely taught many of his or her rights. There are associations and journals that aim to do just that. But the right of a consumer to choose or refuse a product (for whatever reasons) is a basic right, independent of education in these rights.

Understandably, educational institutions such as the university or the museum have not been immune to the growing tension between the pedagogic and performative kinds of democracy. The so-called "culture wars" of the 1980s that saw the canons of the Western academy being both vigorously challenged and defended, the rise of varieties of cultural relativism, the accent on diversity and the politics of identity, the coming of postmodern and postcolonial criticism, have all left their mark on these institutions. These debates around pedagogic versus performative kinds of democracy are inconclusive but it can be safely said that very few, if any, museums or universities will now want to go back to the purity of nineteenth — or early twentieth-century propositions and ignore the discussions of postcolonial, indigenous and multicultural critics. Nor would they want to deny the reality of consumerist practices within which public institutions are situated. But that said, interesting and rigorous debates still take place in particular institutions about the specific mix of the two models of politics with which particular situations should be handled. The ensuing decisions, needless to say, are principled as well as political and pragmatic. They do not offer any universal solutions to our dilemmas but I look on these debates as a reminder of tension between the pedagogic and the performative models of democracy. This tension is what we have to negotiate as we contemplate the futures, in late democracies, of the class of institutions we call "museums".

Like the university, the museum also has had to accept that education and entertainment are not opposed to each other. But museums, for reasons I go into below, have been more affected by the process than universities. They have had to embrace the proposition that their clientele have choice and their preferences need to be addressed; that education will largely have to pay for itself and that state-funding will have to be supplemented by endowments and revenue. Along with this have come debates that have challenged the authority of the museum in deciding what could be collected and exhibited. Museums have been drawn into debates about the past, its representation and ownership, debates often driven by the so-called politics of identity. The last point has been a particularly sensitive one for peoples struggling for forms of cultural sovereignty. Indigenous peoples in various parts of world (including Australia) have successfully challenged the idea that everything could be exhibited to anybody or that scientific curiosity represented a greater human interest than a particular group's cultural use and possession of objects. As a result, museums have also emerged as a key site for cultural politics arising over questions of the past in late democracies.

Museums, democracy and the politics of experience

I want to suggest that if the pedagogic model of democracy privileges the capacity for abstract reasoning and imagination in the citizen, the performative one brings into view the domain of the embodied and the sensual. And that is what makes the roles of visual and other sensual practices different in the two models. Think of the education that once aimed to give the citizen the capacity to conceive of and visualise abstract things, such as the idea of the nation. There were visual aids, of course: maps, statues and other images of national unity. But the way school and university disciplines such as history, geography, political science and anthropology enabled one to think the nation or community was through developing skills for visualising abstractions. I still vividly remember a question a non-literate peasant-girl who hailed from a village in the district of the 24 Parganas near Calcutta once asked me as she accompanied my cousin, her family and myself making our way to Calcutta from Delhi by car in 1973. A domestic maid in my cousin's home, she had lived in Delhi for quite a few years now and been exposed to television and cinema. And yet, a few miles away from Delhi and her curiosity stoked by unfamiliar surroundings, she asked, "Tell me, Dipeshda [my older brother, Dipesh], is Kashmir a part the 24 Parganas?". We all laughed at her "ignorance" of Indian geography, but the incident also told me how much one's geographical imagination was a matter of education and training in visualising — through instruments such as the map — completely imperceptible entities like the nation.

In pedagogic models of democracy, citizenship is based on the capacity for reasoning. This capacity is assumed to stand supreme as the machine through which all information needs to be processed. It is as if the pedagogic model privileges the brain over the senses. The museum of the past would collect and put in juxtaposition objects and artefacts that never belonged together in their natural/cultural distribution in the world. The zoological garden would do the same with animals, and libraries with books. All these arrangements would privilege the conceptual or the analytic over the lived. The zoo would make a catalogue come alive, as it were. Museums and archives — both modern institutions for preserving relics of the past — were close to each other in principle at their moments of origin. Just as the museum curator ignored the sensory aspects of the exhibits, historians trained in the traditions of their science would seldom include in their narratives the tactile or sensory part of their research. The experience of old brittle documents going to pieces in their hands, the smell of old newspapers, the strain on the eye caused by past styles of handwriting, the allergy attacks they might suffer from the dust in the archives — in short, everything that made the so-called relic of the past a part of the lived present as well — would be put to one side in order for the past to emerge in clear distance from the present. Why would the senses be so relegated to the background in the work of the analytic? Because, it was assumed in this way of thinking, that it was only through analytic reasoning that one reached the deeper, general and invisible "truths" about society, whatever they were — class, economic forces, natural laws. That which was merely perceptual, not subordinated to reason — and, in that sense, part of the lived experience — gave us access to only the local and particular.

The analytic, one might say, always wanted to subordinate

"experience" or the "lived" to itself.[5] Yet the realm of experience has asserted itself more and more in academic history or anthropology whenever these disciplines have tried to respond to the pressures of democracy. But not always with happy results. Historians in the 1960s and seventies explored "oral history" assuming that the experiences reported by people would nicely fill out stories available in the archives, and thus democratise the discipline of history without challenging its basic precepts. Instead they found themselves in the land of memories which always blurred the distinction between the past and the present that was crucial for historical analysis and objectivity.[6] A disciplinary unease exists between the field of memory and academic history. Anthropologists have similarly wrestled with strategies to release the lived and the experienced from their traditional subjection to analysis but with mixed results. The reasons are not far to seek. The vision of the political that academic disciplines are wedded to belongs to my first model of democracy: citizenship as the capacity for abstract reasoning. Indeed, without such reasoning, the critical-political edge of the social sciences would be blunted. How would you otherwise visualise as concrete and real such invisible entities as capital, social structure, instrumental rationality, and so on? And without these categories, how would one develop modern critiques of social relations?

Museums, being public places where one does not usually require special qualifications to enter, have been more open to the pressure of mass democracies and have had to address more directly issues of experience. They have therefore also had to be more sensitive to the politics that question the presumed primacy of the analytic over the lived. In his well-known essay "On Collecting Art and Culture", the anthropologist James Clifford gives an early instance of this from the life of the Musée de l'Homme in Paris. He cites an essay published in 1986 by Anne Vitart-Fardoulis, a curator at the museum. Vitart-Farduolis describes how one day a Native American man walked into the museum and suddenly, by talking in a personal and intimate way about "a famous intricately painted animal skin", challenged the primacy of the analytic over the lived:

The grandson of one of the Indians who came to Paris with Buffalo Bill was searching for the [painted skin] tunic his grandfather had been forced to sell to pay his way back to the United States when the circus collapsed. I showed him all the tunics in our collection, and he paused before one of them. Controlling his emotion, he spoke. He told the meaning of this lock of hair, of that design, why this color had been used, the meaning of that feather ... This garment, formerly beautiful and interesting but passive and indifferent, little by little became ... [an] active testimony to a living moment through the mediation of someone who did not ***observe*** *and* ***analyze*** *it but who* ***lived*** *the object and for whom the object lived. It scarcely matters whether the tunic is really his grandfather's.* [7]

I do not have to remind the reader that this Native American man could have walked into a museum in the nineteenth century and said the same things but he would not have been heard. Why do we hear him now? Because the politics of identity — the question of who can speak for whom — are, like it or not, part of the cultural politics of a liberal democracy. The more our attention has turned to the formerly "colonised" within the West, the more anti-colonial themes and questions have come to mark liberal democracies' attempts at multiculturalism. The history of colonialism and of colonial knowledge shows how the universalistic and humanist analytic frames of the social sciences were once used to classify, control and subordinate the colonised both within and outside the West.[8] It was the same process that also resulted in the pre-colonial knowledge systems of the colonised now living subjugated lives, relegated to the supposedly parochial and untheoretical realms of "experience".

Fig.1 Barber shop installation in the ***Digging Deeper*** *exhibition at the District Six Museum Cape Town, South Africa.*
Photo: Haajirah Esau, Copyright: District Siz Museum

It is precisely against such politics of knowledge that the cry goes up from time to time from the ranks of the historically-oppressed, "to hell with your archives, we have the experience!". [9]

In opening themselves up to the politics of experience, museums have gradually moved away from the archives, a modern institution with which they once shared paradigms of knowledge. For the politics of experience orients us to the realms of the senses and the embodied. This is never achieved by the capacity for abstract reasoning. It takes us away from the senses, it trains us to be sceptical of the evidence they produce about the world. University education, on the other hand, can train us, as I have said, to visualise as concrete that which is invisible to the natural eye. But it speaks to (and of) a disembodied subject of history, a position that we individually are called to inhabit when we know the world from that position. The museum of today, however, increasingly opens itself up to the embodied and the lived. It provides as much "experience" as abstract knowledge. And this is directly a part of my second model of democracy.

Let me illustrate this briefly with the example of the District Six Museum in Cape Town, South Africa. As many readers will know, District Six was a well-known "mixed" neighbourhood in Cape Town that was literally bulldozed between 1966 and 1984

Fig2. Exterior, District Six Museum.
Photo Copyright: District Siz Museum

to make it into an area for the Whites. Thousands of people lost their dwellings overnight. Families and neighbours were torn apart and dispersed. The museum grew organically out of the protest movement that fearlessly challenged this brutal act of undemocracy. Started in 1994, the museum developed into a site for communal memory, not a nostalgic monument to a dead past but a living memory that is part of the struggle against racism in post-Apartheid South Africa. Older residents and their children visit the museum to imbibe the memories that inform their present struggles. The museum makes special effort to remember the streets of the neighbourhood. Here is a part of a testimony from one of the visitors to the museum, showing how the logic of remembering, as distinct from that of history, leads inexorably to the realms of the sensory and embodied:

The streets of my childhood in Sea Point survive as the bones of an articulated skeleton remain preserved. On visiting there, my memories jostling, it occurred to me that this act of remembering can be likened to watching a video — in reverse motion ... Around the bones grow organs for living and sometimes flesh ... But the process of remembering is filtered and textured, entangling stages of then and now. It culminates in an evocation of old-new things, rather than the "flesh" of what was once there. A process that is at the same time so intimate and yet beyond our grasp... Along streets we all made our way, linking beacons of home, school and the shop. In a recurring dream verging on nightmare, I pick my way in nauseating dread along the Main Road toward school, bearing a heavy suitcase ... And memories push forward; hot pavements, the scream of seagulls and the droning foghorn, yellow-foaming sea and crackling palm fronds; but the strongest memory-sense of all, the smell of watermelon, permeating from the fresh-cut grass of the beachfront lawns, to the residents of the nearby hotels, flats and scattered houses.[10]

You can see in this quotation how mem-ory, eventually, can never be separated from the domain of the senses, for memory always has elements that are embodied. We cannot even predict these embodied memories in their entirety. This actually produces a paradoxical result for what is often disparagingly called "identity politics". It is true that the politics of diverse identities in democracies often lead people to make indefensible claims connecting experience with identity. For instance, it could be claimed — and often is — that only the members of a particular group have the right or the capacity to understand/represent the group because they have the necessary and requisite experience. Sometimes, as I have already said, knowing particular histories of oppression helps us to empathise with these claims. But the very nature and politics of experience actually belies such claims. The realm of the lived ultimately belongs to embodied existence. And experience always touches on this level. It follows then that experience does not have to always connote a subject (or an identity) defining the experience as such. Experience is not always subjective in a psychological sense, if by psychology we refer to processes that go on only in the brain.[11] The body also has experiences and remembers them. The politics of identity thus often reaches out to a level that actually defeats any project that the "politicians of identity" may have of making identities appear fixed, immutable and essentialised. For who can tell ahead of any event what the mind-body complex may or may not remember? Experience, thus, does not have to speak to a politics of identity.

By opening out to questions of the embodied and the lived, museums address certain formations of the public in modern democracies that academic disciplines do not address. A democracy needs an informed public and public debates. Academic models of knowledge privilege information that, supposedly, the brain processes. These models of knowledge marginalise the senses. Democ-racies have moved on to a variety of politics in which information is not simply packaged for the brain to process; information is now also what addresses other senses — of seeing, hearing, smelling, and touching. In the democracy of the masses and the media, the realms of the embodied are increasingly politically powerful. It is not that the expertise and rationality produced by the traditional academic disciplines are redundant or irrelevant. But their traditional scepticism towards the embodied and the sensory will not help us in understanding why memory and experience — in other words, embodied knowledge — will play as important roles in the politics of democracies as the disembodied knowledge academic disciplines aspire to. Museums, more than archives and history departments, have travelled the distance needed to keep up with changes that mark late democracies.

Endnotes:

1. See the Introduction to Simon During ed., *The Cultural Studies Reader*, (London and New York: Routledge, 1999) for a discussion of these issues.

2. Homi Bhabha, "Dissemination: Time, narrative and the margins of the modern nation" in his *The Location of Culture*, (London and New York: Routledge, 1994), pp. 139-170.

3. Geoffrey Gray, "From Nomadism to Citizenship: A P Elkin and Aboriginal Advancement" in Nicolas Peterson and Will Sanders eds., *Citizenship and Indigenous Australians: Changing Conceptions and Possibilities*, (Cambridge: Cambridge University Press, 1998), pp. 55-76.

4. For a discussion of the complexities and ambiguities of the 1967 referendum in Australia, see Bain Attwood and Andrew Markus, "Representation Matters: The 1967 Referendum and Citizenship" in Nicolas Peterson and Will Sanders (eds), *Citizenship and Indigenous Australians: Changing Conceptions and Possibilities*, (Melbourne: Cambridge University Press, 1998), pp. 118-40.

5. See the last chapter to my book *Provincializing Europe: Postcolonial Thought and Historical Difference*, (Princeton, New Jersey: Princeton University Press, 2000).

6. Joan Scott's much-cited essay, "The Evidence of Experience", in *Critical Inquiry*, 17, Summer 1991, pp. 772-797, reproduces, this time with a post-structuralist suspicion of the subject, the social analyst's scepticism about the usefulness of "experience" as a guide to social realities.

7. Vitart-Fardoulis cited in James Clifford, "On Collecting Art and Culture" in his *The Predicament of Culture: Twentieth-Century Ethnography, Literature, and Art,* (Cambridge, Mass.: Harvard University Press, 1988), p. 246. Emphasis added.

8. Bernard Cohn, *Colonialism and its Forms of Knowledge,* (Princeton, New Jersey: Princeton University Press, 1998) is a classic statement of some of the issues involved here.

9. I discuss this more in my essay "Globalization, Democratization, and the Evacuation of History?" in Jackie Assayag and Veronique Benei (eds), *East in West*, (Delhi: Permanent Black, forthcoming).

10. Lalou Meltzer, "Past Streets" in Ciraj Rasool and Sandra Prosalendis (eds), *Recalling Community in Cape Town*, (Cape Town: District Six Museum, 2001), pp. 21-22.

11. Joan Scott's essay "The Evidence of Experience" seems to make this assumption.

Public Culture and the Future of History

The study of popular culture has always presented historians with methodological challenges that have sometimes led to a considerable amount of rethinking of disciplinary protocols. Today's popular culture is more like what Carol Breckenridge and Arjun Appadurai once called "public culture", if by such an expression we refer to the very close connection between the media and the production of "culture" that has marked the last hundred years. What I want to hazard here are a few speculations about the relationship between public culture and the future of the academic discipline of history.

When History became a professional discipline in the West towards the middle of the nineteenth century, it necessarily developed close ties to the written word. Historians came to look upon certain written texts as their "primary" sources. Archives were the institutions that housed such documents. The very idea of institutions that would serve bona fide research scholars by giving all equal access to documents meant that, logically and historically, archives would develop as public and state-owned institutions. Indeed, when Sir Jadunath Sarkar worked with others to set up the Indian Historical Records Commission in 1919 as an important part of the archiving movement in India, he would often emphasize the "public" (and hence state-owned) nature of the archives that would collect both government and private records, catalogue them, and hold them in the interest of research in Indian history. Much, however, has changed since Sir Jadunath's days, and particularly so since the Second World War. The rise in the popular demand for a more democratic and decolonized world has resulted in significant, if implicit, revisions to historians' ideas about archives. As the discipline enlarged its brief from around the time of the War to make the everyday lives of "ordinary" people one of its principal interests, it also had to widen the concept of "archives" and to find new ways of reading them. Since "ordinary lives" do not leave documentary trail in the quite the same way as do the lives of the political, military or social elite even in societies that have the tradition of writing, historians have been forced to look far beyond their own discipline in search of evidence. Information relating to material culture, cultural practices, oral and other non-written forms of remembering has engaged their attention. One can think of G. D. H. Cole and Raymond Postgate's *The Common People* (1938) as one of the books that pioneered this trend towards making the non-elite the subject of history. Nearer home, the Bengali historian Niharranjan Ray's magnum opus *bangalir itihash (A History of the Bengali People*; written in the nineteen forties but recently translated into English by John Hood) could be assigned a similar position in Indian history.

Cole and Postgate concentrated on "political and economic aspects" of the life of the "common people" from the late eighteenth century, deliberately omitting any discussion of "art, literature and science." In other words, they did not quite study "popular culture"; the economic and political information they looked for could be easily had from official archives. Ray, on the other hand, made ideas, art, literature, and the material culture of the Bengali people central to his exercise. His idea of the archives also was correspondingly wider. He mined textual, inscriptional as well as information about archaeology, physical geography, and numismatics to make reasonable guesses about how Bengalis who did not constitute the elite may have lived in the past. It is, of course, entirely reasonable that as one delves into pasts for which written primary records are unavailable that one should look to other disciplines to provide clues about where such pasts may have been, in a manner of speaking, archived.

Even for periods for which written records are otherwise available aplenty — such as the period of the rise of capitalist institutions in Western Europe and elsewhere — the subject of popular culture, rural or urban, has always presented challenges to historian. It has been one thing to reconstruct the institutional history of modernization or "early modernity" in different societies, but where would one go to find out how, for example, workers "experienced" such modernity if they have not left us diaries, literature, or autobiographies? Historians have responded to such tasks with impressive creativity, thus helping to renew the discipline. Eugene Weber, Keith Thomas, Edward Thompson, Robert Darnton, Natalie Davis moved towards anthropology; Davis and Carlo Ginzburg developed the field of microhistory (something that may also describe the later work of the *Annales* school); Greg Dening, Marshall Sahlins, Rhys Isaac, Donna Merwick, Inga Clendinen and others led the way towards ethnographic history. Jan Vansina, working out of the African context, showed us how one might read oral traditions to reconstruct the past. Ranajit Guha, in studying "insurgent consciousness" among peasants in colonial India in the nineteenth century turned towards structuralism and semiotics to look for tools that might unlock the mysteries of insurgent practices. The emphasis that Thompson and Hobsbawm and others of their generation — and then the feminists too in the nineteen seventies — placed on the importance of recovering marginalized people's experience of social change, led naturally to the development of "oral history". Paul Thompson's book, *The Voice of the Past* (1978) captures the spirit of this movement. Oral history proved enormously helpful in examining the pasts of not only urban working classes or peasants but of tribal and indigenous peoples as well.

But even these steps had some unforeseen consequences for our ideas regarding archives. What once looked like an intelligent and simple move to look beyond traditional archives ended up in some cases raising new questions about one might think of the archive itself. For example, "oral history" did not necessarily yield information that nicely filled gaps in the archives and complemented what was available in the written sources. Historians came to realize that oral history was more about memory than about the past that is available in documents. Memory did not so much complement as it supplemented written sources. That is to say, instead of simply filling gaps in written sources, memory both supplied what was missing in the latter and by the same token called attention to the limits of such sources as well. By the nineteen eighties and nineties, it was becoming clear that memory and history did not line up into a neat Indian file. Memory was both sought and found, as Paul Ricoeur points out in his recent book on the subject; it included both remembering and forgetting. A lot of memory, in addition, could be involuntary. In South Asian studies, the works of Shahid Amin on Chauri Chaura, Ajay Skaria on the pasts of Dangi Bhils, of Ritu Menon, Urvashi Butalia, Kamla Bhasin, and Gyanendra Pandey on the Partition and its memories — one could no doubt adduce other examples — directly address the question of how oral history might altogether differ from disciplinary history. It was thus as if popular culture, with its emphasis on memory and orality, recorded the traditions of popular life in ways quite fundamentally different from the constitutive principles of the official process of documentation, though, as Shahid Amin usefully reminds us in his *Event, Metaphor, Memory* (1995), the popular and the official are always in dialogue with each other.

Just as the study of pre-cinema and pre-television popular culture once revolutionized historians' ideas regarding practices and institutions for archiving the past, we may very well be at a similar juncture today with respect to the future of the discipline of history. What if a historian came along in a hundred years' time and wanted to write histories of our own, contemporary popular culture? What would be the repositories of popular culture now? Today's popular culture borders on mass culture in probably every part of the world. It has been — and is being — profoundly influenced by cinema, television, video and the internet and all other growing paraphernalia of the electronic world. This is not to say that it is the same all over the world. Indeed, it will be the job of historians to explain why, in spite of the global influence of the media, popular culture differed from one part of the world to another; or how, ironically, globalization sometimes helped to create the politics of big, global differences (between the so-called West and Islam, say, according to some extremists on both sides). But however the story is told, the role of the media is going to be critical in it.

If this is true, then it follows that the historian of the future will be much more of a media-analyst than the wordsmith he or she is today. The future historian of the twentieth century and later will need training in understanding how the media works, how visual and sound-effects, and not just words, produce political arguments and persuade people. Can post-war nationalism be understood without taking the media into account? So much of global politics today — the politics of truth and reconciliation in South Africa, of the controversial business of saying "sorry" to the Aboriginals in Australia, of reconciliation of war-time memories between Japan and Korea or China, the two wars in Iraq — is inconceivable without the media. Institutionally, I already see the beginnings of the scholarly response to this situation. We now have students who want to produce multi-media Ph.D theses (it catches my generation of scholars on the wrong foot, for we don't have the skills needed to evaluate such dissertations). We now have on hand a younger crop of sports and cultural historians who are most attentive to the role the media play in connecting the local, the national, and the global. The "Sarai" group of scholars at the Centre for the Study of Developing Society in Delhi and those associated with the Centre for the Study of Culture and Society in Bangalore — to give but two examples — appear to be experimenting in this direction. In the field of Indian history, we have the case of Ravi Vasudevan who actually, ahead of his time, took the trouble to train himself in methods of both film and historical analysis. In short, I see the gap between historians and analysts of the media narrowing in future and doing so of necessity, not to speak of the fact that the future historian will be much more computer-literate than people like myself for whom the computer is still a glorified typewriter. The future historian, in general, will belong to what the American historian Robert Rosenstone has called a post-literate world. The post-literate are not illiterate. They are those who can read but won't, for they are reared on the media and are much more comfortable expressing themselves through them.

This is not to say that the "traditional" historian as who have come to know him or her will be extinct. But it is to say that historians of contemporary popular culture will have to engage with media studies with the same degree of seriousness with which the social historians of Thompson's generation engaged with Cultural Anthropology. They will in turn have new problems to do deal with. The close connection between popular culture and the digital work will present new problems of data storage and retrieval. The problem is not only the tremendous proliferation of information that the electronic world creates. The problem also is the ironically ephemeral nature of this data. Historians who have started to study electronic archives are already reporting a significant loss of information from its having been stored in formats that become obsolete with rapid advances in technology or from the prohibitive costs of translation from one format into another. The electronic form of storage may well turn out to be more ephemeral than the oral forms found in many societies, both past and present. A Panini or the Vedas could be orally transmitted undistorted for hundreds of centuries but the same may not be true of electronic transmission. The future historian using the media as archive may have to cope with institutional and technological forms of forgetting that are themselves quite new. The field of memory-studies may thus in turn have to be recast.

This is where, as a historian, I see the importance of the collection of short essays being presented here. Scholars who study different aspects of the media-molded popular culture of today are laying the foundations for a transformed discipline of history tomorrow.

Where Is the Now?

I want to speak to two concerns that are visible in many of the comments circulated: the tendency to understand the present as a guide to the future — a historicizing endeavor — and the concern about being political (that is, working out the social purpose of criticism). Robert Pippin quotes Hegel's *Philosophy of Right*: "Philosophy is its own time comprehended in thoughts"(p. 425). Criticism is not the same as rigorous philosophy. But it is, in our case, infected with the spirit of that statement from Hegel. Criticism must reflect its own time. It has to both interpret and speak to the world. That is the condition for effective critique. Critique has to figure out the now. "To live in and work for our century", is how Catharine Stimpson puts it (p. 436). Our commentators share a concern about being able to name, designate, and describe the time or period we are passing through.

Most of the comments assume a certain definition of the present. Science and technology are critical to this definition. Tom Mitchell's provocative opening questions set the tone: has "theory" become "therapeutic" and timid faced with "rapid transformations" in the media, biotechnology, and in the logic of capitalism itself (pp. 330, 331)? Whether or not theory has become timid, many commentators agree with Mitchell's understanding of the present. Hansen points to the conditions created by "the unprecedented acceleration of circulation and technological innovation with the advent of technological development, its power to destroy and enslave" (p. 394). Jerome McGann, Elizabeth Abel, Lorraine Daston, Stimpson, J. Millis Miller, and others advocate engagement on the part pf the humanities with these new developments in science and communications technology and even beyond them into the realms of economics, rational choice theory, primatology, and so on.

The periodizing instinct and the political instinct are deeply connected. "To the extent that it [thinking] is invested in figuring out the now — that is to say, the enigma of the world," writes de Lauretis, "the thinking of theory is political" (p. 365). How we periodize our present is thus connected to the question of how we imagine the political. The reverse must be true as well: that every imagination of the political entails a certain figure of the now. That is why, when we begin by defining the now in a very particular way as our first step of anarlysis, we have in a sense already committed to ourselves to certain understandings of the political. These very understandings themselves, however, may need to be more interrogated than assumed.

The statements from the members of the board treasure the ideal of a deliberative democracy in which university-based humanities academics play the role of public intellectuals with the aim of furthering the causes of social justice and democracy. Harry Harootunian thus explains the social-political use of theory: "What *Critical Inquiry* might do ... is to provide a forum for the recovery of theory's true vocation as a condition for beginning the difficult labor of trying to envisage a discourse on modernity that speaks to the world outside the academy" (p. 401). Even Mary Poovey's cautious call for a more rigorous *Critical Inquiry* that remains confined to academia — "writing to each other (and for our students) is OK" — envisages a transcendental, albeit academic, public that acts as a repository of a "collective understanding of what it means to be human" (p. 433). Poovey's caution is well taken, but her statement begs the question of the political, for what divides even an academic "collective understanding" of the meaning of being human are our different and colliding normative visions of human collectivities. And that is where the political comes in even if the academic-public intellectual is always situated at a distance from the writer in the mass media. Surely, the popularity of poststructuralism, deconstruction, and postcolonialism in the seventies and eighties owed itself, to some degree at least, to the expectation that these theories would only make our democratic imaginations ever more vigorously democratic. Think of

Foucault's insurrectionary preface to *Anti-Oedipus*!

Yet what — coming as I do both from an imaginary West and from somewhere outside of it — I find a little troubling in our statements is our readiness to assume that both the now and the political are easily divined. It is as if all that *Critical Inquiry* needs to do is to find forms of practice adequate to our divinations of the present and the political. I read Harootunian's description of "theory's true vocation" from two contradictory perspectives. A split informs my sense of the present. It is somewhat like the negative condition that Pippin describes in his statement but with a different programmatic implication.

The split consists in this. The normative pictures of a modern society that I carry inside my head are, typically and necessarily, European or Western in origin. I think through an intellectual tradition in which one is able to spell out, at least in principle, the broad constitution of a just social order on an a priori basis (Marx on the Gotha program and Rawls on justice would be examples of this). I use this blueprint to critique existing inequities. Yet I recognize that there are political imaginations shaping popular politics all over the world today that escape or exceed our normative understanding of the political. These imaginations belong neither to the Left nor to the Right. But they have global implications for governance